TARGETED TACTICS®

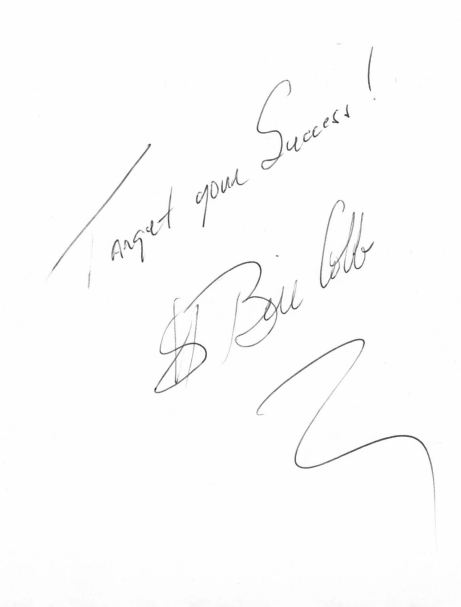

Target your Success !

Bill Cobb

TARGETED TACTICS®

Transforming Strategy

into Measurable Results

William R. ($Bill) Cobb

Library of Congress Control Number: 2007901304
ISBN: Hardcover   978-1-4257-4990-3
                 Softcover   978-1-4257-4989-7

This book was printed in the United States of America.

To order additional copies of this book, contact:
Xlibris Corporation
1-888-795-4274
www.Xlibris.com
Orders@Xlibris.com
35417

CONTENTS

For the incredible women in my life,
Maureen, Kelly, and Kim, love you, guys.

ACKNOWLEDGMENTS

Charles M. Lillis, PhD, for showing the way; Bill Jacobson and Mariano Delle Donne for their insightful comments; Kelly, Skip, Kim, and Todd for their invaluable perspective; and W. Mitchell for always being there to pick me up whenever I stumbled.

PREFACE

Businessmen love numbers. Numbers make them feel secure . . . As they grow, corporations tend to lose this feel for the market . . . they start to manage by the numbers. Managers begin to worry about the efficiencies of mass production and less about the needs of the market. Managers must maintain their intuitive feel for market trends and attitudes. They should look at the numbers, but they shouldn't be ruled by them.

—Regis McKenna

My colleagues and I share a common concern that we are losing sight of the marketing disciplines required to sustain our institutions. We seem to have become preoccupied with numerical reporting instead of managing the growth and development of our businesses, and as a result, we have allowed too many scorekeepers and not enough practitioners into our management ranks. As a result of this trend, we are lacking in problem solving skills, and the value-added component of insightful leadership seems to be on the decline. If this trend continues, we will be in danger of losing our global competitiveness and the stability of our cherished institutions. We should not allow this to happen, and we need to reinstate the management practices and critical marketing disciplines that were prevalent when these institutions were originally created.

In the opening chapter of the *Marketing Managers Handbook,* Edward Bursk, professor of business administration of the Harvard Graduate School of Business, and William Morton, president, International Marketing Association Inc., reminded us of the challenges marketing professionals are facing in today's increasingly complex world. They offered ten reasons in support of the need to strengthen the marketing discipline and improve the processes we apply to executing this function. I have taken the liberty of adding two additional reasons to their already-compelling list and suggest that we need to remain aware of the following:

1) The buying-and-selling relationship is a subtle, fluid interaction between two people (multiplied by the hundreds or thousands), and those on both sides continually affect each other.

2) Those on the buying side are so many and so various and so far out of the direct control of the seller that the seller has to rely on persuasion to lead them. Yet persuasion itself can never be 100 percent applicable to all the people—far from it!

3) The seller has at his or her command and therefore must choose among a whole array of possible ways and combinations of ways to affect the buyers that he or she is trying to persuade.

4) The information at the seller's disposal is, at best, so imperfect that he or she can never be more than partly sure how prospective approaches will work, particularly since the market that he or she is going to deal with will be changing as the result of those particular efforts.

5) General conditions are continually changing, both in terms of economic forces and social trends, so that even what is attractive when it is on the drawing board may have lost its appeal by the time it reaches the market two or three years later.

6) Every seller has competitors who are always trying to outguess and outmaneuver him or her, often deliberately taking action just to spoil their carefully planned efforts.

7) Now that buyers, the public, live comfortably above the level of physical needs, competition is broadened. Every seller must contend not just with rival products of the same kind, but with rival uses for the same money.

8) Differences between rival products and rival uses of money have become more difficult to discern and more psychological in nature, thus putting an extra premium on the penetration and persuasiveness of the selling. Differences that otherwise would be barely noticeable can be made stronger in the buyer's eyes by the efforts of the seller.

9) Because of the state of competition, it has become more difficult for many individual firms to continue to grow. In the effort to reach certain customers more directly, traditional channels of distribution have become scrambled. Companies find themselves using mixes of wholesalers, retailers, etc., bypassing others, and they sometimes end up competing with some of their own customers.

10) Another disturbing trend is that costs have been so dramatically cut that organizations wind up diluting their sales focus and spreading their sales effort across a multitude of product lines, particularly for products with fewer unique features or differentiation. This has increased their promotional costs, and as a result, margins have deteriorated to the point where there is not much leeway in which to make marketing errors.

11) Investments in mechanization, and correspondingly the effort to move large quantities of products out into the market, have created more opportunity for the small business to find a market among the buyers who have become dissatisfied with standard products and services. This can make it more expensive for large business to be off target just a little when aiming at mass markets and depending on volume.

12) Global trading has introduced a whole new set of competitive conditions as overseas engineering and manufacturing costs can be considerably lower, and patent and intellectual property rights are not always rigidly enforced.

These twelve observations sum up the fact that today's marketing problems deal with more subtle and complex variables. This calls for a more systematic and analytical approach to managing the marketing process, and this was the motivation for developing the Targeted Tactics® program and writing this book. Over the course of my career, I have had to meet these challenges in a number of different operating environments, and although the enterprise content has always varied from company to company, the marketing disciplines that needed to be followed were remarkably the same. I am confident in making that statement because the teams I led were successful whenever we applied these disciplines, and conversely were not when we shortcut the process.

I am now known as an "experienced professional," which means that I am approaching the last stages of my career. I have had the privilege of holding some very challenging assignments over the years and have worked for many different kinds of organizations from fledgling start-ups to large established institutions. As a result of this experience, I have gained a real appreciation for the complexities of the business environment. Even the best of ideas will fall short in any organization if the resources that implement them are not appropriately aligned and integrated. This simple concept seems to be overlooked most frequently in our larger institutions, because their size and complexity will often create segregated operations that disguise what is actually taking place within their ranks.

I spent a good portion of my career within these larger institutions, working in those middle management positions that exist between *strategy* and *results*. This has often been referred to as the middle ground within an enterprise where "the rubber meets the sky" and "the rubber meets the road" collide. It is that critical implementation space within all organizations where the strategies that are approved and funded actually turn into plans, activities, and results. Or to be more precise, this is that critical implementation space within all institutions where the strategies that are approved and funded *should* turn into plans, activities, and results.

The individuals who shoulder these responsibilities are typically division general managers, marketing vice presidents, market managers, and product managers all charged with the responsibility of growing the enterprise. I have great respect and appreciation for these professionals because I know firsthand how difficult this challenge can be. I have been charged with all of these responsibilities at one time or another in my career and, through this experience, discovered that there are very few published road maps to help any of us achieve the desired results. There are many excellent publications that address specific elements of what is required, but none that I am aware of that integrate each of these piece parts into a definitive process.

As a practitioner, I am suggesting that to be proficient with any marketing program, we can always benefit from a little practical experience. There is no better way to gain that experience than to walk through the market fires and get burned on occasion, and I assure you that I have actually been there and done that. Experience still remains life's greatest teacher, and the things that I have had to learn the hard way have served to create a good portion of the content for this book. This manuscript is a *Reader's Digest* compilation of those lessons learned, and I offer it to you as a resource to help you gain from this experience. Will Rogers said it best: "You might as well learn from the mistakes of others, because you probably won't live long enough to make them all yourself."

This publication has been written for the middle managers, the men and women who are given the stretch objectives, limited resources, and *have to figure out how* to obtain their organization's challenging new growth projections. We will assume throughout the book that we have just attended one of those infamous planning sessions where the C crowd (CEO, COO, CFO, etc.) have just presented the annual business plan. The plan includes a requirement to double our market share from 10 to 20 percent in five years. This elite C group will now return to their duties of managing the stakeholders, allocating resources, and babysitting the organization. We, on the other hand, have now got to find a way to develop new products, extend product life cycles, enter new markets, acquire new customers, and stretch our resources to accomplish this new objective. How are we going to do that?

INTRODUCTION

We tend to confuse marketing effectiveness with sales effectiveness. This is our big mistake . . . and in the end, it hurts sales and the total business. If the sales force does not have the right products to sell, know their best prospects, and have a viable value proposition to offer, their energy counts for little. Market based thinking is not easy to introduce into an organization. It tends to be misunderstood or, once understood, easily forgotten in the wake of success. Marketing is characterized by a law of slow learning and rapid forgetting.

—Peter Kotler

Every business strategy has to start with an idea or a concept that satisfies a market need. It may address an established market need, it may address an emerging market need; it can even address a hidden market need, but at the end of the day, someone has to have a need to purchase something from someone, or there is no business, period! This very fundamental belief is the foundation of a management system called market-based management. It requires that all strategic and operating decisions to be based on an understanding of how they will be received within the economy, an industry, a market segment, or by a customer group.

I was first introduced to market-based management in the middle 1980s by Charles M. Lillis, PhD, who at the time was the chief planning officer for US West, one of the Regional Bell Operating Companies. Dr. Lillis raised our organization's level of consciousness by focusing the planning and operating choices we considered on specific markets and customers with similar needs. As the result of this direction, US West restructured its marketing approach to form market units that were dedicated to these defined customer groups. We subsequently offered our entire suite of capabilities through these dedicated channels, resulting in a collection of market units that were more closely aligned with their customers. Each was organized to meet their customers' specific requirements and ultimately measured on how well they served their client base.

I was given the assignment to manage the federal government market unit. The federal government was our largest retail customer at the time, but the federal government was about to privatize their communication requirements. They announced that they would be putting their communication systems out for competitive bid, and this meant that a significant portion of the revenues we were presently enjoying were about to leave our network and our business. We had never experienced anything quite like this prior to the break up of the Bell System, so we were ill prepared to deal with this new marketplace reality. We had to develop a new marketing strategy to try and win back our largest existing customer.

We formed an unregulated federal government contracting subsidiary to compete in this new environment. We had to learn how to prepare competitive proposals, operate within the federal governments contracting guidelines, and then implement these contracts under a whole new economic model. Fortunately, we did figure it out, and we recaptured a significant portion of these revenues for the firm. Our new market focus enabled us to discover new and different kinds of opportunities as well, and we went on to leverage this new contracting capability in creative ways. As a result of our broadened market focus, we were now able to compete for different kinds of contracts and in new geographies. We eventually established ourselves as a private virtual network provider in addition to being just a public network operator.

The point of sharing this example is not to brag about our good fortune (or good luck), but rather to point out the benefit of a market-based approach. If US West had not refocused its resources around their customer groups, we may not have even been aware that these market changes were taking place. We would not have formed a new subsidiary to compete for the federal government's business; and as a result, we would have sustained a significant decline in revenues from our largest customer. Granted it meant changing the way we did business within this market space but by adapting, we were able to sustain our market position.

Building on knowledge of the market enables an organization to focus its decisions in ways that directly impact customer relationships. Products and services are developed to take advantage of competitive differences; operating decisions are made in support of customer requirements, and operating results are directly tied to the satisfaction of customer needs. It all starts with acquiring knowledge of the market, the market segments that are going to be addressed, and then an understanding what the customers within these segments expect.

Market Based Management*

Operating Results

Operating Decisions

Competitive Advantage

Market & Market Segment Selection

*Acknowledgement: Charles M. Lillis, Ph.D.

Through this real-life example, we can readily see the benefits of employing a market-based management approach. It enabled US West to understand where opportunity was moving within the market. Once that fact was recognized, US West was then able to identify the characteristics of the changed opportunity and, as a result, could focus the business resources to capitalize on this knowledge. The benefits of taking this approach at a minimum enabled US West to do the following:

- Be better able to see market changes at the earliest possible time by being closer to the market environment
- Gain the ability to see more opportunity as we become more closely aligned with our customers
- Gain the ability to more clearly ascertain and leverage our differential advantage
- More effectively manage cost as we refocused resources more deliberately
- Be better able to discriminate in terms of the investments and product choices we were making

Sadly, many of the core marketing disciplines are being regularly overlooked in today's business environment and being narrowly defined with such things as variations of the four Ps (product, packaging, pricing, and promotion)—or worse yet, spin-doctoring and advertising. Marketing is actually much more than that; it is the process of identifying a need, describing the requirements to fulfill that need, developing a product or service that meets those requirements, and then managing the presentation of that product or service to a set of customers that will derive a benefit from it. It is very difficult to do it well, and yet it is the very foundation for every business enterprise.

Because the market environment changes constantly, applying a consistent analytical process to these dynamics is highly desirable. Taking this approach will enable us to identify and quantify market changes as they are taking place. If we do not apply a consistent approach, then we risk not only missing these market changes, but more importantly, we risk not making the necessary adjustments to react to them. It is in this area that the larger institutions continue to struggle as resource constraints, short budgeting timelines, and lack of awareness often prevent this process from reoccurring. To help organizations refresh their skills, we will be introducing a tool called the marketing concept cycle. The Targeted Tactics® program employs this tool as its very foundation, and then adds to it a series of processes and methodologies to help institutions implement the concept. This combination of strategy and tactics enables us to identify, target, develop, manage, resource, and measure an effective marketing effort. We are adding the *how* to the *what* so that we will have a framework that can be applied to our own industry and specific company needs.

As we begin to examine the various phases of the program, it is important to recognize that each phase can be and should be addressed differently depending on the size of the organization. For example, in phase 1—"Determining Marketplace Environment"—we will examine the planning assumptions that are normally addressed by strategic planning groups within the larger institutions. Within smaller organizations, this is an area that the owners will often address, as it is usually the very basis for the establishment of their business enterprise. For our purposes, we just need to gain an understanding of the business climate and how our organization fits into this environment. It is an important data point to help us shape the tactical plans we intend to develop and implement.

In phase 2 of the program—"Decide Nature of Company's Business"—we will discover another arena that usually gets a lot of attention from the planners and owners of the business. In the development of our marketing plans and programs, we will not be trying to change these fundamental judgments. What we will be seeking to do is better understand them, and then explore what other capabilities we could or should develop if we find that we have a need to do so. Our hypothetical challenge will be to grow revenues and market share, so we will want to know what our present capacity is and what our future capability needs to be.

Beginning with phase 3 of the program—"Identification of Customer Set"—we will be delving deep into the disciplines that marketing practitioners are traditionally responsible for. We will be addressing the process for targeting customers and identifying market segments. We will suggest generic approaches to segmenting markets and qualifying targeted buyers. We will also look at different buying behaviors, buying characteristics, and buying decision processes for different market groupings. We will be introducing methods and techniques to help us find out who and where our potential customers are. Knowing who our customers are, where they are, and how they buy is absolutely critical to the success of our market plan.

In phase 4 of the program—"Determine Product and Sales Strategy"—we will discuss the fundamentals of product planning, product development, and product management. We will introduce the concept of product mapping and a process for identifying potential product voids. We will follow this with a method for selecting distribution channels for our products, and some additional thoughts on how to effectively manage them. You will find a good portion of the content of this manuscript is focused on phases 3, 4, and 5 because it is here where the rubber really does meet the road. If we cannot identify the right markets, target the right customers, position the right product sets, and select the most effective channels, we are never going to achieve or sustain market success.

In phase 5 of the program—"Organize and Apply the Resources"—we will actually develop our goals and the organization needed to execute our plan. We will address the challenge of resource allocation and the alignment of our marketing organization to support the effort. Although it is impossible for us to consider every conceivable scenario, we have tried to introduce some generic concepts to help work through these issues. We will provide a listing of the traditional marketing functions and some suggestions on how to outsource certain marketing disciplines or activities. The goal is to establish our goals and implementation plans around those opportunities that give our companies the best chance for success.

In phases 6 and 7 of the model—"Monitor and Measure Results" and "Feedback"—we deal with the quantitative and qualitative elements of executing our plans. We have deliberately avoided the traditional views encountered in this arena because the accountants and scorekeepers will always address those needs. What we have elected to introduce in their place is visibility into the levers and gauges that impact the financial measurements and influence their outcome. We believe that if we pay attention to the right things, the numbers will take care of themselves. We want to measure what can affect the results, not just report the results.

As we work through the program, you will undoubtedly observe that the marketing concept cycle is a cycle; it is not static. It is deliberately designed to continuously repeat itself in order to address the constant ebbs and flows of marketplace dynamics. This is why we chose it as the foundation for the Targeted Tactics® program, and we are going to add to it the benefit of experience and implementation techniques. As we complete each phase of the program, we will be recommending a checklist of activities that evolve from the effort. Our goal is to complete the cycle and, as a result of doing so, produce a market plan that enables our organizations to be successful.

Marketing is still perceived as somewhat of an art, not a science, but a scientific approach needs to be considered when we are building our market plans. The scientific reasoning process strives to predict an outcome of an event by understanding the things that impact or effect that outcome. We are also striving to predict an outcome, albeit a revenue prediction, and we need to identify all of the variables that impact and contribute to that outcome as well. The Targeted Tactics® program will provide you with a methodology and the tools to do just that.

In the military, the field level commanding officers don't get to pick their battles; they are just required to win them. Those of us who are employed in these middle management assignments don't get to pick our assignments either, but we are also required to accomplish them. In order to do so, we will need intelligence (market data), reconnaissance (competitive information), armament (products and services), a plan of attack (targeted markets and customers), troops (resources and skills), communications (measurement systems), and a way of determining whether or not we have achieved victory (feedback).

Marketing Concept Model

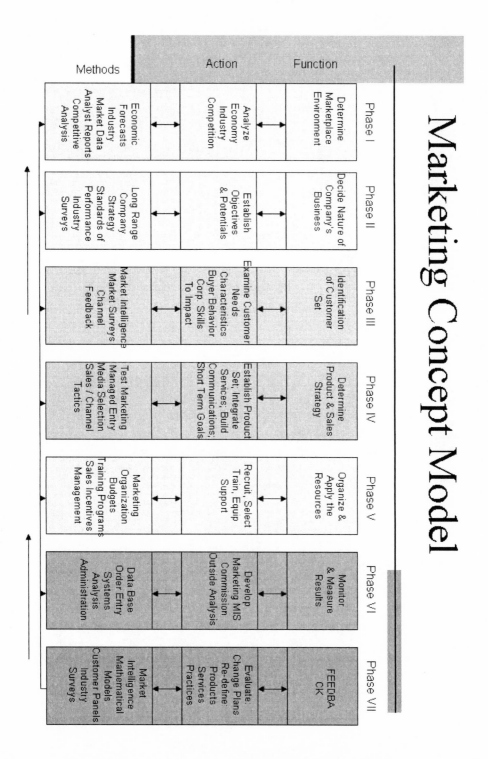

	Function	Action	Methods
Phase I	Determine Marketplace Environment	Analyze Economy Industry Competition	Economic Forecasts Industry Market Data Analyst Reports Competitive Analysis
Phase II	Decide Nature of Company's Business	Establish Objectives & Potentials	Long Range Company Strategy Standards of Performance Industry Surveys
Phase III	Identification of Customer Set	Examine Customer Needs Characteristics Buyer Behavior Corp. Skills To Impact	Market Intelligence Market Surveys Channel Feedback
Phase IV	Determine Product & Sales Strategy	Establish Product Set, Integrate Services; Build Communications; Short Term Goals	Test Marketing Managed Entry Media Selection Sales / Channel Tactics
Phase V	Organize & Apply the Resources	Recruit, Select Train, Equip Support	Marketing Organization Budgets Training Programs Sales Incentives Management
Phase VI	Monitor & Measure Results	Develop Marketing MIS Commission Outside Analysis	Data Base Order Entry Systems Analysis Administration
Phase VII	FEEDBA CK	Evaluate; Change Plans Re-define Products Services Practices	Market Intelligence Mathematical Models Customer Panels Industry Surveys

Determining Marketplace Environment

You've got to be very careful if you don't know where you are going, because you might not get there.

—Yogi Berra

The purpose of phase 1 of our program is to gain an understanding of the environment we are going to compete in. We will not be challenging the business strategy decisions that have already been made by others but rather preparing ourselves to do our jobs more effectively. If we are going to enter the arena, we have to know what the game is, how they keep score, and who it is we have to compete against to win. No more, no less.

There are a minimum of four components to the intelligence we require, and we need to gain insight into each of them in order to understand our environment. First is the economy; second is the industry we are part of; third is potential disruptions (such as changes in regulation or technology); and fourth, the competitive landscape within our market segment. Any one of these four influences can have an effect on the success of our market plan, so we want to become familiar with them. We are being asked to double our market share over the next five years, so we want to understand what the playing conditions are like. This is the very first phase of creating our market plan, and it is where we acquire the information that will eventually become the basis for our assumptions and beliefs.

We are assembling information at this first phase of the program that will become the foundation for our market plan. The C crowd does not want to hear that their strategies and objectives are unattainable, but rather want to know what is required to successfully implement them. We are going to make general statements about our environment in this phase of our market planning that considers the following:

- The economic indicators that we believe are relevant to our business interests and the forecast for these indicators
- A definition of our industry and market segment we will be competing in along with any current projections and forecasts
- Any change or proposed change in regulation or business practices that could affect our product offerings or our business
- Any new or disruptive technology that could impact our product plans.
- The identification of our major competitors and a representation of their current market position and known strategies or direction
- A calculation of our market share in relation to these same major competitors in order to benchmark our current position
- A reference to one or more credible "stack ranking" publications that represents our current position within the industry as perceived by others

The Economy

Our planning document is going to assemble and evaluate the economic indices that are relevant to our industry and our business interests. We will want to point out applicable historical trends and any future projection for our segment of the economy. Our intent is to discover whether or not these economic conditions are going to remain favorable, or change, while we accomplish what we want to do—grow our enterprise. The US economy has always experienced business cycles, and it is more practical to plan on growing during periods of economic expansion than during periods of recession.

Whenever we suggest to the operating managers that they pay attention to this element of their plan, we are always confronted with some degree of resistance. They are quick to point out that the economy is outside of their control, so why worry about it? There are very valid reasons why we should pay attention to these indicators, as there are portions of the economy that are relevant to everyone's business interest. These economic forecasts are going to become the equivalent of our weather report, and although it will not change what we are setting out to do, it could influence how we prepare to execute.

The US Department of Commerce does an excellent job of assembling and disseminating economic data (www.census.gov). There is information for consumer markets, industrial markets, government markets, and information on foreign trade. Their Bureau of Economic Analysis (www.bea.gov) assembles and reports economic data on the gross domestic product, personal income, and annual industry accounts by industry sector. They track the US balance of payments, international investments, and information about international trade. They also provide regional economic accounts by gross state product, state personal income, and state per capita personal income. We can determine trends for who has the money and where the money is moving just by examining these web sites.

We can also visit the Federal Reserve Web site (www.federalreserve.gov) and learn more about economic forecasts and changes in monetary rates. The Federal Reserve bank offers additional information on capacity utilization, consumer credit, flow of funds, and the cost of short—and long-term money. It is a worthwhile exercise to track the effects of changes in monetary policy, as it will have an effect on things such as capital spending for infrastructure, purchasing patterns and production capacity expansion decisions, consumer credit (which impacts retail sales), housing starts, and the purchase of related durable goods.

The important thing to be cognizant of is that there truly are some things outside of our control. We can track those elements that affect our business interests via the US Department of Commerce Economic Indicators Division (www.economicindicators.gov). They release eighteen different economic sector reports on a regularly scheduled basis. They also provide historical trend information that can help us determine if our segment of the economy should continue to be favorable over the course of our planning period. Just because we can't control these factors, doesn't mean we can ignore them. We just need to adjust our strategies and tactics to accommodate changes when they are incurred.

As practitioners, we don't need to chart and predict the health of the entire world economy. We just need to know where to go and what to look for to develop our plans.

Let's look at the consumer segment of the economy and imagine that we are in the personal services business. This business is represented by the services segment of the economy, which is growing at a 3-percent rate per annum, and represents about 41 percent of the dollars spent for personal consumption. This segment of the economy is expected to continue to grow at a comparable pace to the gross domestic product and remain in its relative position with respect to its importance to the consumer. This tells us that the economic factors that we contend with are going to remain reasonably steady and that our success or failure will not be impacted by unforeseen economic dislocations.

If we are in the industrial segment of the economy, then our interests will be in corporate earnings and the overall financial health of these industrial institutions (corporate profits). We would be pleased to learn that our domestic industries have consistently improved earnings from a collective $672.2 billion in the year 2000, to $1,133.7 billion in 2005. If we are in the chemical products sector of the economy, then we would discover that earnings for our industry have improved from $14.2 billion in the year 2000, to $45.3 billion in the year 2005. We will choose to track these indicators at the NAICS (North American Industry Code) code level so that we can monitor the economic health of our targeted market segments. Our assumption is that these indices are representative of the *health* of our business interests and that we will want to remain aware of any major change within them throughout the planning period.

If we are serving the government markets, we will want to highlight planned government spending over the course of our planning period. We will discover that the federal government will be increasing its current spending levels from its 2006 level of $2,472 billion to $3,053 billion in 2010. We may choose to identify specific categories that apply to our service offerings and interests as well. If we are planning on serving the state and local government sector, then we would want to assimilate comparable information about their planned expenditures.

Our goal is to identify those economic factors that could impact our marketing efforts one way or the other. If there is an economic slow down, then we may slow our expansion plans. Conversely, if the economy expands more favorably than we anticipate, then we have the option to accelerate. Our summaries should communicate the status and trends of the economic factors that impact our business. Whether our economic forecast is for sunshine or rain, we will still have to go outside and compete; we may just need to *dress* differently.

US Dept. of Commerce, Census Bureau

United States
Census
2000

AMERICAN COMMUNITY SURVEY
~ America's Changing, So Is the Census ~

Population Clocks
U.S. 299,475,421
World 6,534,670,995
22:04 GMT (EST+5) Aug 14, 2006

People & Households	Estimates · American Community Survey · Projections · Housing · Income | State Family Income · Poverty · Health Insurance · International · Genealogy · More
Business & Industry	Economic Census · Economic Indicators · NAICS · Survey of Business Owners · Government · E-Stats · Foreign Trade | Export Codes · Local Employment Dynamics · More
Geography	Maps · TIGER · Gazetteer · More
Newsroom	Releases · Facts For Features · Minority Links · Broadcast & Photo Services · Embargo Request · More
Special Topics	Hurricane Data and Emergency Preparedness · Census Calendar · Training · For Teachers · Statistical Abstract · FedStats · FirstGov

The Industry

Once we become familiar with these economic data points, we will want to establish our relative position within our own specific industry (market share and industry ranking), how big our industry is in total, and how fast it is growing. Since we are being challenged to gain market share, we have to develop a set of tactics to accomplish that goal. If we are going to need to enter new markets, then that will create one set of tactics. If we are going to have to capture market share from existing competitors, that would require a different set of tactics. One size does *not* fit all, and our operating choices must support the desired outcome.

An industry is defined as a group of firms attempting to satisfy a particular need within a market or market segment. We want to develop an assessment of how well our industry is doing as a whole and how well we are all expected to do in the future. What we are seeking to discover is the collective economic prediction that either allows for our continued expansion or potential disruption. What is important to us is not only the overall forecast for the financial health of our industry, but also the relative position each of the participants holds within the industry.

At the macro level, our friends at the Department of Commerce report industry data on construction, manufacturing, mining, retail trade, services, transportation, wholesale trade, international trade, and government activities. We are going to want to break this down further into specific industry groupings, and we can do this by industry code—NAICS or Standard Industrial Classification (SIC). We can also rely on third parties to assemble this information for us, as many financial firms, commercial banks, and investment bankers follow specific industries and assemble this data on a regular basis.

If our current organization does not assemble this kind of information, then we will need to obtain it on our own. We can choose to rely on trade publications, professional associations, and industry associations to help us acquire this kind of information. We can also go to the investment community and obtain copies of industry sector reports, which are the same reports that are available to commercial investors. I have had to rely on these sources many times during my career, and they usually provided a totally unbiased perspective. Industry data can also be acquired from trade journals, commercial research reports, and market research firms such as Frost & Sullivan (www.marketresearch.com).

There are other sources out on the Internet as well, and one of the easiest to use is Business Miner (www.bizminer.com). They can help us to research our business interests by industry clusters, then major industry groupings, then segment further down to individual industries, and finally down to our specific segments within an industry. They provide business statistics for both marketing and financial information, and they get to a very impressive level of detail. They presently maintain information for seventeen thousand industries in over three hundred market areas, and can break it down on a state-by-state basis where applicable.

If we were seeking to research our industry position within the consumer market for our personal services example, we would discover that there is information available on 553,628 firms. On average, these individual professional services firms bill $260,808 in revenues every year, and as a collective total generate approximately $135 billion in revenues. About 17,898 new firms start up each year, of which almost 22 percent experience difficulty and wind up failing within their first three years. From this kind of information we can determine the size of the industry ($135 billion), the number of competitors we could face (550,000 plus), our relative position with respect to the participants (our total revenues vs. the aggregate $135 billion). If we chose, we can even look deeper and determine the geographies where we could experience the highest concentration of competition.

If we are a provider of data processing services, we would discover that this industry continues to experience robust growth. There are, as of 2002, 13,789 companies in this segment—up from 7,588 in 1997. Total revenues during this period were $53.7 billion—up from $30.8 billion in 1997. The industry is growing at a rate which almost doubles every five years. Once again, from this information, we can determine the total size of our industry ($53.7 billion), our relative position (our total revenues divided by $53.7 billion), and the number of competitors we could face (13,789). We are simply trying to understand how big the pie is, how big it will be in the next five years, and what our position needs to be.

If we are a government contractor or simply concentrating our efforts within this market segment, we are going to want to know what the government is planning to do. We want to know how much money they are going to spend on those activities that are related to our business interests. The best source for government spending information for the federal government is the Office of Management and Budget (www.omb.gov), and there are comparable reporting groups within each of the state governments. The budget is public information, so we can research each of the identified spending categories and determine whether planned expenditures are growing or declining for our particular area of interest. There are also government publications available (e.g., government executive) that will also provide government spending information by different categories, and some agencies will even identify their priorities and programs for the coming fiscal period.

Federal Government Spending Information

OFFICE OF
MANAGEMENT AND BUDGET

Budget Overview
Funding Priorities, restraining other spending...
Economy
Ensuring Prosperity for Future Generations...
Science and Space
Expanding knowledge through research...
Health Care
Increasing access to affordability...
Homeland Security
Protecting the Nation...

FY 2006 and FY 2007 Supplementals, Amendments, and Releases

If we choose to engage our own market research firm to help identify these facts, then we need to be clear about their research responsibility, what they intend to provide, and, equally important, what we are willing to accept. Our requirement for their services is going to be periodical, not continuous, so we want to make that point clear. We will engage them to produce specific information that answers a set of marketing questions that we define so that there is no misunderstanding as to what it is we are trying to learn from their efforts. The real value of utilizing our own research firm is that we can address the specific issues that are important to our business interests and have an established set of reference points to measure our plans and programs.

We want to qualify their research personnel, preferring more of the academic and analytical approach over an intuitive approach. We want to set and insist on a specific budget to accomplish the work. We want them to provide a schedule of interim reports that enables us to view and interpret their progress toward meeting our research objectives. And finally, we will insist on an agreement that clearly states how the research is going to be used. We have no intention of buying marketing research that is going to be resold to others, particularly to our competitors. The selection of a firm and the information requested needs to be in line with the size and requirements of our organization.

We will be restating the industry's growth projections that have been provided from these independent sources and benchmarking our current industry position. We will assume as part of our hypothetical challenge that we have a 10 percent share of a given market or industry and that this market is expected to continue growing at 10 percent per annum. In order for us to meet the growth challenge we have just been given, we will need to increase our share from 10 to 20 percent within the next five years. We are now confirming where we are (with respect to others within our industry) and where we want to be in the next five years (also in terms of our desired industry position).

Potential Disruptors

In addition to understanding the overall size of our industry and its expected growth rate, we are going to want to pay attention to any major changes taking place within it. For example, are there new technologies or applications of technology that will impact or change the way the industry designs and develops new products? Are there new business practices being introduced that affect warranty and exchange policies? Are there new financing schemes being offered that will cause our current clients to change their buying positions? We want to identify and be aware of any disruptive market forces that could impact our future plans.

Technology just won't stand still, and keeping abreast of its evolution is part of what we are asked to do. Those of us who come from the information technology industries are very familiar with Moore's law, which basically reminds us that computer chips get smaller and smarter with every generation. These chips are now being integrated into nontechnology products, and we are about to be inundated with everything from "smart appliances" to even "smarter automobiles." The new Lexus commercials have just announced that they have an automobile that can parallel park without any assistance from the driver, a real distinct advantage when you have to take a driver's license test.

If you do not believe that change is accelerating at an alarming pace, consider the following facts: there are now over eight hundred million personal computers on the planet, one for every seven or eight human beings. The estimated number of Internet users is between eight hundred million and a billion. Alvin and Heidi Toffler, in their latest publication *Revolutionary Wealth,* pointed out that in 2002, the Japanese built a computer called the Earth Simulator, designed to help forecast climate changes. It performed four trillion calculations per second. They went on to further explain that by the year 2005, a computer at Lawrence Livermore National Laboratory was capable of one hundred thirty-six trillion operations per second. Scientists are now predicting that computers may reach petaflop speeds, a thousand trillion mathematical operations per second by the end of this decade.

If we look back at the twentieth century, we were inundated with more disrupted technologies and changes than at any other point in the history of man. We transitioned from steam engines to jet engines, from vacuum tubes to computer chips, from paper to plastic, from telegraph to telephone, and countless numbers of other transitions, including the discovery of nuclear physics. We can't predict what may be in store for us in the twenty-first century; but we do know that in fiscal year 2005, inventors applied for 409,532 new patents. Of them 165,485 were subsequently approved, and that leaves a whole bunch more pending. Somewhere out there is something that will eventually change the way we do business. Recognizing how these new capabilities could add value to our existing products and services is part of our job.

If our organization does not have a research and development group or a professional engineering staff, then staying current with these developments will be more challenging. Industry trade publications do publish breakthroughs, and competitors are even quicker to announce their new developments. Investing in professional trade journals is an alternative for staying in touch, as well as subscribing to a notification service that tracks new patents or licensing agreements. We do not have to care about all of the advancements taking place in every area, but we do want to be aware of any new developments that could affect our business interests. These new discoveries will eventually have an impact on our future product plans and new product development choices.

Business practices can also affect our market plans as changes in the way our competitors offer and support their products will influence our market environment as well. Consider the exchange practices of Nordstrom's, the well-recognized and renowned retailer. Nordstrom's will allow its customers to return or exchange any purchase, with virtually no questions asked. There are even rumors of shoppers returning things to Nordstrom's that they didn't even purchase there. This policy has had a dramatic effect on how other retailers now need to structure their return and exchange policies. If you are colocated in a shopping mall with Nordstrom's, you are going to be expected to behave like Nordstrom's.

The classic example of this kind of change in business practice is the story of Chrysler Corporation, and it occurred during their well-publicized turnaround years led by Lee Iacocca. Mr. Iacocca had to do something dramatically different to convince the American consumer that Chrysler Corporation had resolved its product quality issues. He took a very bold step in introducing the first five-year warranty program, which was previously unheard of in the automobile industry. This has subsequently changed the way that the entire industry operates ever sense, as multiyear warranties are now commonplace throughout the automotive industry.

For whatever the reasons, regulation does not stand still either. The individuals we elect to public office do their best to react to the needs of society and, on occasion, feel obligated to interfere with the dynamics of free enterprise. Their interest and intent are usually sincere, and their motives are to protect us from ourselves. For example, none of us would argue with the need to have a Food and Drug Administration that does its very best to ensure that the things we ingest won't cause us harm. These government bodies are constantly reexamining their methods and practices and will change the rules when they fell they have discovered a reason to do so.

What we want to be sure of is that we are aware of these rule changes. If we have a new requirement to adapt a product or product line to meet a new safety requirement, we want to identify this as part of our environmental assessment. If we are given a new financial reporting requirement (e.g., Sarbanes-Oxley), we want to understand the operating and cost implications of compliance. If the office of consumer affairs has identified a business practice that we should be concerned with, we have to know about it as well. We will be relying on others within our organizations to help us stay abreast of these issues.

The Competition

In every planning cycle, the strategists and analysts will make an effort to identify the competitive landscape. Planners and tacticians see this world very, very differently. The strategists will talk about generic capabilities, market positions, and the probable strategies these competitors will elect to follow. They will draw market maps and populate them with vectors that show that someone is moving into someone else's market space and that company A is seeking to acquire company B as a means to enter these different segments. They plot these activities in a very similar fashion to the way that Pentagon generals map adversary military movements.

But the military field commanders and we, marketing practitioners, are looking at those movements from an entirely different perspective. In order for us to compete against our adversaries, we will need to understand their strengths and their weaknesses. We should not expect to get this information from the planners. We will have to develop our own competitive profiles and incorporate them into our execution plans later on in the program. What we are going to want to know is the following: their logistics—where do they operate?; their products—what do they offer?; their alliances—who are they working with?; their customers—where will we encounter them?; their channels—how they go to market?; their fulfillment approach—how they service and support their products?

For now, we want to identify who is the current market leader, who is getting stronger, and who is struggling. This is critical information for us because when we put together our tactical plans we may not want to challenge the market leader but rather contest one of our weaker competitors. We want to know what the current share of the market is for each of these identified competitors and be cognizant of any new plans or developments they may be considering. We will also try to anticipate any new entrants who may be considering entering the market or any existing competitors that may be considering exiting the market.

We will establish where we stand in relation to our identified major competitors. Not just in terms of market share, but also in terms of customer perception. This is often a hard matrix to measure; but industry trade publications traditionally take surveys, and they often rank different organizations with respect to quality, ease of doing business, overall reputation, etc. We are going to be challenging ourselves to increase our share of the market, and we may need to improve our stature within these industry rankings to accomplish this. Our belief is that we can achieve this result, although we are going to be relying on support from other parts of the organization to enable the accomplishment of this goal.

Whatever industry reports we elect to use to determine our industry position, we just need it to be consistent over the life of the planning period. We can start with the most notable ones, the *Fortune* 500 (by *Fortune* magazine) listings, *Inc.* 500 (produced by *Inc.* magazine annually), and the *Forbes* listing of the largest privately held companies. Gartner Dataquest annually announce the top ten information technology service providers, and *Federal Computer Week* ranks the top twenty-five system integrators. *Government Executive* ranks the top one hundred federal technology contractors, the top twenty-five NASA contractors, the top overall two hundred federal contractors, and top one hundred defense contractors. We just need to pick the list that makes the most sense for us.

Industry forecast data can be provided from multiple sources. It can come from the planners or third parties, or from the research we initiate. To validate our position within the industry, we need to understand the factors that will determine our ranking: our annual revenues, our products, and our competitive position. These factors will constitute our industry ranking, and it is important that the whole organization start with the same points of reference. Our hypothetical challenge is to grow revenues and double our market share, so we need to validate our current market position and our present industry ranking as our baseline.

Marketing is a competitive practice, and we will be met with resistance in the market, particularly if we are trying to take market share away from someone else. The better prepared we are to compete, the better we will compete. Trying to compete without having a basic knowledge of our environment is at the very least foolish and, at the worst, comparable to walking into an ambush. We are going to target our tactics to coincide with anticipated economic trends and validated industry opportunities. We are going to identify our targets of opportunity and compete where our chances for success will be most favorable.

In the analogy of our military field commander, we now have our intelligence and reconnaissance reports. We want to make sure that the C crowd understands what it is they are asking us to do in terms of revenue growth and market share gain. We also want to make sure that they understand the conditions under which we will be accepting this challenge (the economic conditions and competitive landscape). We are going to confirm our current and desired industry position as it relates to our major competition. From this very basic statement of our desired goals and objectives will come our tactical planning, our specific goals and objectives, our financial requirements, and our organizational needs.

Phase 1 Deliverables

We need to construct a statement that fairly represents our place within the economy. We should be able to state that we are part of the X sector of the economy that has been consistently growing at Y percent for the last n years. We participate in the Z segment of this sector, which is expected to sustain this growth rate over the course of our panning horizon. These conditions are favorable/unfavorable to the achievement of our market plans.

Sources of information:

- US Department of Commerce (www.census.gov)
- Bureau of Economic Analysis (www.bea.gov)
- Department of Commerce Economic Indicators Division (www.economicindicators.gov)
- US Federal Reserve bank (www.federalreserve.gov)
- Regional and local banks

We need to construct a statement that represents the parameters of our particular industry, its size, and its growth rate. We should be able to state that our industry is growing at X percent and is expected to be $Y within the next five years—our planning horizon. We anticipate that we can capture X percent of this market over the course of the planning period that will enable us to achieve our new growth objectives.

Sources of information:

- US Department of Commerce (www.census.com)
- Financial analyst sector reports
- Specific industry associations
- Specific industry trade publications
- Third-party research publications
- Contracted research firm

We will need to identify any new or proposed regulation that could impact our present plans or product direction. As part of this review, we will also seek to identify any new or disruptive technology or change in business practices that could have an impact on our existing or proposed product plans.

Sources of information:

- Government publications and public policy forums
- Our legal advisors (internal or external counsel)
- Universities and national laboratories
- Professional and technical publications
- Research reports and industry publications

We must also identify the major competitors that we will encounter in the execution of our plans. We do not need to know all of them, but we must recognize the top three to five that hold a significant position within the marketplace. We are going to be measuring our progress against these major players so that we can determine our relevant position as the result of our efforts.

Sources of information:

- Financial analyst sector reports
- Industry trade publications
- Industry trade associations
- Third-party research publications
- Contracted research firm

Our goal in phase 1 of our program is to be able to construct a two—or three-page summary of our assumptions and beliefs about the environment our organization is going to compete in. Ideally, we paint a picture that says the economic conditions are good, our industry is growing, our market niche is clearly identified, and the competitive landscape is known. Knowing where we want to go and how quickly we want to get there is the first step in developing our plans and organizing our efforts.

Phase 1 Checklist

- We know where we fit within the economy and its outlook.
- We identified new regulation, technologies, or business practices.
- We know our industry, how large it is, and its projected growth.
- We know our major competitors and our relevant position to them.
- We have identified the market position we are striving to achieve.

Decide Nature of Company's Business

Get your facts first, and then you are free to distort them as much as you please.

—*Mark Twain*

The purpose of phase 2 of our program is to help us understand what we have to work with, what it is we may need to add or acquire, and where we may have to invest in order to attain our newly assigned growth objective. We begin our organizational assessment by examining four major categories of our existing business plan: our current product plans, our current channel relationships, our core competencies and capabilities (skill sets), and our organization's capacity to expand. We are going to be making assumptions about what our business-as-usual scenario will produce and what it is we will have to do differently to meet our new growth challenge.

It is critical that we communicate openly and honestly throughout this next phase of the process, as more often than not; the areas of the organization that will become strained from an aggressive marketing effort do not reside within marketing's span of control. For example, engineering, production, warehousing, fulfillment, order entry, billing and settlements, and servicing organizations are all going to be significantly impacted by aggressive revenue growth. If any part of the organization is unprepared to support these new requirements, then the market plan will not succeed.

As part of our market planning, we are going to establish our market position with respect to who we are, what we do, and how well we do it. So this phase of the program needs to consider the following:

- Establishing a formal definition of what we do and where it fits into our industry and our market niche
- An inventory of our existing products and services, identifying those products approaching their sunset
- An examination of our existing sales channels relationships and an estimate of their capacity to sell and support additional volumes
- Discussions with our operations and production teams to assessed our capacity to meet our new growth requirements
- An inventory of our current skills and capabilities, recognizing areas for potential improvement to support our aggressive expansion plans

Remember, we are still in the data gathering stage, and the acquisition of this knowledge will help us to formulate the tactics we will need to implement. Although we will discuss additional options for products and channels further in phase 4 of the program, for right now, we want to document what it is we are presently doing.

Products

We begin by reviewing our current product plans. We are going to list all of our existing products and services, and document where they are in their respective life cycles. Some may be still be in the early stages of maturity and can provide incremental growth opportunities for our firm. Others may have reached the end of their usefulness and are about to be replaced by a newer generation or emerging substitutes. Recognizing this is a good thing, as we will want to address this as part of our future product planning and consider the need to develop replacements. What we want to recognize is the effect that these different life cycle factors could have on our aggressive new growth plans. We have to a need to sell more of something, so we are engaging in a process to determine what that something needs to looks like.

Product Life Cycles

Life Cycle Stage	Market Characteristics	Resulting Strategies
Product Introduction	Few competitors Potential buyers uninformed Low price elasticity Low volume / Higher costs	Develop widespread awareness Large trade discounts Heavy promotion campaigns Exclusive distribution
Product Growth	Entry of aggressive competition Early adopters enter market Rabid increase in sales volume Reduction in production costs	Establish strong distribution niche Full line pricing – normal discounts Emphasis on selective demand Increase distribution / inventories
Product Maturity	Shake out of marginal competition Late majority & replacement buyers Decline in sales growth rate Beginning of profit squeeze	Maintain & strengthen loyalty Styling & design improvements Defensive pricing / discounts Emphasize service elements
Product Decline	Fewer competitors Final adapters arrive & purchase Declines in sales volumes Competition from substitutes	Attempt to sustain margins Abandon smaller market segments Frequent price concessions Minimize promotional costs

If we are employed in a very large company that offers hundreds of products and product variations, this is going to be a significant undertaking. This task will need to be broken down into smaller, more manageable product groupings, and then each of these groupings will need to be broken down further into individual product sets. Our data collection needs to document the name of the product, its current life cycle position, its current unit price, unit cost, and resulting gross margin. We are going to be entering this information into a tool that we call the mother of all matrices. This matrix is going to become our integrated database and it will help us to discover untapped targets of opportunity for potential new revenue growth.

If we do not have an organizational structure that supports the collection of this data, then we are going to have to employ some sort of enterprise search technology (data mining), to capture this information. Collecting this information from various divisions, product areas, and different sales channels can be very difficult. There are companies that can handle this kind of challenge, and the one that I recommend is called Knowledge Webb (www. knowledgewebb.com). Knowledge Webb has developed a technology called Aubice ™ that can facilitate the mining of this kind of data from disparate databases within large enterprises. They also provide the capability to sort these findings so that we can transfer it to our mother of all matrices for analysis.

Our mother of all matrices is going to continue to grow in size and complexity as we add to it other elements from the program. Initially, we are going to populate it with our business-as-usual data—what it is we are currently providing and how it is being priced and supported. As we continue to move through the various stages of the Targeted Tactics® program, we will be adding other components of the marketing mix to the matrix, such as proposed new products, sales channels, and promotion schemes. For now, we are just documenting what we currently sell.

Our first vertical column is going to list all of our identified products and services. Next, we are going to add additional columns to reflect our current sales price and direct costs for each of our products or product categories. We will want to allow for variable calculations within these cells so that we can change pricing and cost as part of our future product planning. Capturing this initial starting point is essential because it represents our current product plans, our product life cycle predictions, and their present value to our firm. We have to document unit pricing, direct unit costs, and the resulting unit gross margin each product contributes. We have now developed the product plan database for our business-as-usual model for us to analyze and manipulate.

"Mother of All Matrices"

Product Groupings	Life Cycle Stage	Unit Price	Unit Cost	Gross Margin	Promo Cost	Channel Cost	Contribution Margin	Current Plans
Product A	Introduction	$200	$150	$50				
Product B	Growth	$300	$200	$100				
Product C	Growth	$450	$300	$150				
Product D	Maturity	$250	$175	$75				
Summary								
Product E	Decline	$200	$180	$20				
Product F	Decline	$175	$160	$15				
Product G	Decline	$150	$140	$10				
Summary								
Product H	Maturity	$125	$100	$25				
Etc., etc.	Maturity	"N"	"N"	"N"				

If we are a services company, we do not escape the need for participating in a comparable inventory process. We have to document what our service offerings and capabilities are. If we are a systems integrator, we would be totally dependent on the skill sets of our associates and their capacity to remain current with changes in technology and applications. Our services matrix would then look different than a product matrix, but it would address the same issues. Our product line is our ability to provide different application needs, so our products are the different things that we do. Staying current with changes in technology and the application of newer technologies is the equivalent of introducing an enhanced line of product offerings. We have to "productize" these capabilities.

Next we are going to try and capture a snapshot of our current advertising and promotional plans and the expenditures we are making for each of these product groups. At this early stage of data collection, we are primarily interested in how many dollars are being spent in support of each product category. If we our company does not track this on a unit basis, and most of us don't, then we should allocate a cost factor based on our estimate as a percentage of revenues. This will result in us adding yet another vertical column to our mother of all matrices for advertising and promotion. Later we will be challenging ourselves to pool these dollars and reallocate them differently across multiple market segments, so understanding how big the pool is and where it is currently being spent is helpful.

"Mother of All Matrices"

Product Groupings	Life Cycle Stage	Unit Price	Unit Cost	Gross Margin	Promo Cost	Channel Cost	Contribution Margin	Current Plans
Product A	Introduction	$200	$150	$50	$12			Heavily Promote
Product B	Growth	$300	$200	$100	$12			Increase Distribution
Product C	Growth	$450	$300	$150	$18			Increase Distribution
Product D	Maturity	$250	$175	$75	$7.5			Improve Packaging
Summary								
Product E	Decline	$200	$180	$20	$2			Exit Market
Product F	Decline	$175	$160	$15	$1.75			Exit Market
Product G	Decline	$150	$140	$10	$1.50			Exit Market
Summary								
Product H	Maturity	$125	$100	$25	$3.75			Re-price
Etc., etc.	Maturity	"N"	"N"	"N"	"N"			Re-price

A predictable outcome of any product inventory will be to conclude that there may be many more products we could or should offer. We will formalize these discoveries a little later on in our process, but for now we are just trying to determine what it is we presently have to work with. Product voids will be addressed in phase 4 of the program when we begin integrating our targeted market segments with our planned product offerings. Right now, our objective is to get all of our current and planned offerings identified and populated into our mother of all matrices.

Channels

In our hypothetical challenge, we are being asked to rapidly expand the business to a higher level, and we have to determine if our current marketing system can accommodate this incremental request. We need to determine if our existing sales channels can provide expanded geographic coverage, handle larger volumes, or support different kinds of products if we need them to. It is equally important to understand the actual cost of using these channels at both our present and anticipated levels. We are going to be looking at this cost factor in proportion to the revenues these channels generate and the contribution value of the products they handle. Collecting this information is going to require us to add another vertical column to our mother of all matrices so that we can record these cost considerations. Sales channels, fulfillment and logistics, order entry, and customer service all need to be looked at from a larger volume perspective.

We may discover that some of the channel relationships we have in place are capable of handling higher volumes and more complex products. This is a good thing, but each of our existing contract relationships will have to be modified to address our new needs. We could also discover that many of our existing channel relationships will not be able to meet these new requirements. We should identify these weaknesses as part of this internal review process so that we can address the issue in phase 4 of the program where we evaluate our channel selections. We need to anticipate that we will be setting a higher level of expectations for each of our selected channels, and then count on them to meet these new requirements.

For now, we are just trying to determine whether or not our existing distribution system will support our new requirement for accelerated growth. We are documenting the number of channels we have in place, the geographies or vertical industries they address, and the current cost of using these vehicles. We will now add our next column to our mother of all matrices that recognizes the cost for this activity. Our matrix has been expanded once again and now contains our current product plans, our advertising and promotion costs, and our channel or distribution costs. We have created a visual representation of these fundamental marketing mix elements and have built a structure that enables us to understand and vary the relationships between them.

"Mother of All Matrices"

Product Groupings	Life Cycle Stage	Unit Price	Unit Cost	Gross Margin	Promo Cost	Channel Cost	Contribution Margin	Current Plans
Product A	Introduction	$200	$150	$50	$12	$10	$28.00	Heavily Promote
Product B	Growth	$300	$200	$100	$12	$15	$73.00	Increase Distribution
Product C	Growth	$450	$300	$150	$18	$22.5	$109.50	Increase Distribution
Product D	Maturity	$250	$175	$75	$7.5	$12.5	$55.00	Improve Packaging
Summary								
Product E	Decline	$200	$180	$20	$2	$4	$14.00	Exit Market
Product F	Decline	$175	$160	$15	$1.75	$3.5	$9.75	Exit Market
Product G	Decline	$150	$140	$10	$1.50	$3	$5.50	Exit Market
Summary								
Product H	Maturity	$125	$100	$25	$3.75	$5	$16.25	Re-price
Etc., etc	Maturity	"N"	"N"	"N"	"N"	"N"	"N"	Re-price

Earlier in my career, I held a position that managed a national group of independent distributors for a company called Executone Inc. Executone designed and produced electronic telephone systems and relied on this group of independent distributors to sell and service its products. As the business continued to expand, we discovered that the entrepreneurs who owned these distributorships either didn't want to or couldn't accommodate our increasing demands for aggressive growth. We did an assessment of these independent channels and concluded that for our company to achieve what we set out to accomplish, we would have to somehow address this limitation.

We knew that we had to do something differently, so we decided to totally revamp our distribution strategy. We began to purchase our larger distributors and convert these independent businesses into company owned and operated stores. This resulted in a dramatic increase in revenues within these acquired markets, as well as a noticeable improvement in overall customer satisfaction. We were now able to select the management teams for these major market operations as well as provide the necessary working capital support required for growth.

This change in direction created the need to establish a whole new operating division within our company. We had to appoint an executive vice president to run these company operations and establish a new set of distributed control processes and procedures to accommodate this new business activity. Some of the individuals within our organization, who had previously supported these distributors, were reassigned to run these newly acquired company owned stores. When it was all said and done, we created more revenues, more jobs, and better opportunities for many of our associates.

This real life example emphasizes the value of analyzing an existing business practice to evaluate its capacity to support future plans. If, as a result of this process, we should discover a weakness in our distribution channels or in our fulfillment and logistical support, then our planning and budgeting documents need to reflect the required actions necessary to make them better. Business as usual can only support business as usual. We were just challenged to grow our business dramatically, and that will require us to do something different. We must be prepared to make changes if we need to!

Capability

We are going to want to know what capabilities we have to work with to help us achieve the new growth objectives we have just been assigned. We need to determine what the building blocks are imbedded throughout the organization that can be called on to do more. We are trying to establish how we (the collective we) are going to be able to compete against the key competitors we identified in phase I. We have just been asked to grow our business at twice the rate of the industry (27 percent or more per annum) and double our market share from 10 to 20 percent in five years. We need to know whether or not we have the team to accomplish this; and if not, what positions do we need to go out and draft.

To help us sort through this process, we have captured some skill categories to consider and suggest the creation of skills matrix to help us identify and evaluate our current capabilities. Some examples of the things we should look for are

- Management systems, how we govern and control our operations
- Technical competency, our understanding of the different components and applications used in our products

- Customer relationship management, how well we interface with and service our client base
- Overall business acumen, our ability to acquire favorable agreements with business alliances
- Distribution management, how effectively we manage our sales channels
- Product development, how quickly we can identify and productize our ideas
- Project management, how well we implement complex tasks and assignments
- Process management, our ability to integrate different business activities to provide a seamless, error free, customer experience

Understanding what we have and comparing it to what we may need will identify the gaps or areas for improvement we need to address. Since we want to understand better what it is we are good at, it is appropriate to take a look at the skills that our organization possesses. Our perspective will be different than the one that a human resources function would undertake. The personnel function is interested in inventorying individual skills, based on education and experience. We, on the other hand, are seeking to inventory organizational skills, what it is we do well together as a company. So our matrix is going to look a lot different.

Competency Discovery

Skill Set	Poor	Average	Excellent
Management Systems			X
Business Acumen		X	
Technical Competency		X	
Customer Relationship			X

In conducting our organizational analysis, we will seek to formally identify and recognize our company's core competency. Firms that are very established in their fields have had years to develop their core competencies and are exceptionally good at them. For example, for 3M, it's adhesives; for Kellogg, it's food processing; for IBM, it's information management, and so on and so forth. Recognition of this basic building block is important; it helps us to define the universe in which we are able to compete. It is this core capability that is going to allow us to design and develop new products and services, so we have to know what it is. Everybody's products or services started out as a generic concept that evolved from their core competency.

The other benefit to putting ourselves through this exercise is that we may discover that we have more ability than we give ourselves credit for. As we begin to formulate our market plans, we may have a need for additional products and services, or an added capability to reach newly identified market areas. So, understanding not only what we presently do is worthwhile, but recognizing what we could potentially do is even better. Having untapped capability is a competitive advantage and being able to release it within our planning horizon is a bonus. We will later on in the program identify the necessary skills and capabilities we need to expand, so we have to know whether or not we already have them.

This skills matrix will vary from industry to industry, company to company, but it should become part of our thought process for the resource and staffing adjustments that we will address in phase 5. Our goal for now is to be able to define our business, recognize our current capabilities, and discover what we may need to add in order to accomplish our new goals and objectives. We are eliminating any identity crisis we may have.

Capacity

Our next challenge is to conduct a capacity assessment of the organization to identify any limitations or restrictions preventing our aggressive growth plans. Every organization has limitations, and it is important that these discussions take place across the entire management team. As we begin to formalize our market planning, we will be identifying the kinds of products we intend to offer and the number of product units the team is going to have to produce, handle, support, and service. These specifics are going to be different for each individual company, but things will most likely look different for us.

In preparation for our expansion effort, our organization will need to examine

- Our infrastructure (general management, financial capacity, etc.)
- Our human resources (recruiting, retention, development, etc.)
- Our technology assets (intellectual property, R&D, etc.)
- Our purchasing power (material access, cost competitiveness, etc.)
- Our inbound and outbound logistics capacity
- Our operations and assembly capacity
- Our service and support systems
- Our marketing and sales organizations (marketing mix elements)

Remember, our hypothetical challenge is to double our market share in five years, which translates into a significant increase in activity for every function within our company, so we need to prepare.

Capacity Assessment

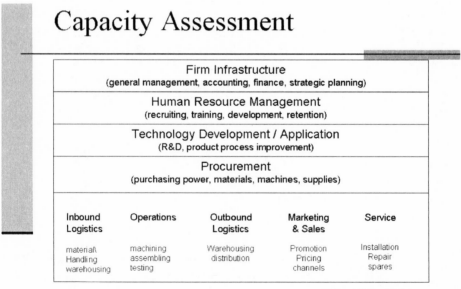

Firm Infrastructure
(general management, accounting, finance, strategic planning)

Human Resource Management
(recruiting, training, development, retention)

Technology Development / Application
(R&D, product process improvement)

Procurement
(purchasing power, materials, machines, supplies)

Inbound Logistics	Operations	Outbound Logistics	Marketing & Sales	Service
material\ Handling warehousing	machining assembling testing	Warehousing distribution	Promotion Pricing channels	Installation Repair spares

Michael Porter Model

We refer to this overall inventory of the company as assessing our firm's expansion capacity. Remember those scorekeepers I referred to in the preface of this manuscript? They are the individuals who inevitably either overlook or ignore all of these new requirements and assume that the growth will just occur. Changes will have to be made to our product plans, our marketing organization, and our support structures. The only way that our organization is going to achieve the sustainable growth we are seeking is to create the expansion capacity necessary to develop and deliver the higher volumes of products and services. There are no shortcuts!

We are working a process that will enable us to recognize the different components we will need to assemble in order to accomplish our growth plans. Our objective is to determine which of these capabilities we currently have and which ones we will have to improve or acquire. We will be making reference to the fact that other segments of the organization will need to prepare as well in order to support our new market plan (engineering, production, accounting, information processing, warehousing, etc.), and that these incremental needs should be considered within their functional planning and budgeting processes. We are going to provide an estimate for these requirements, but we are not yet far enough along in our plans to be specific. That will come later.

The planners and C crowd have a reasonably good understanding of what these needs could be; but once again, we are starting to align our marketing tactics with the total organizations plans and objectives. We have just made others aware of the elements that could directly influence our revenue efforts, so now everyone knows what we all have to consider. We are requesting these different functional groups to recognize and prepare for what they need to do to support our marketing effort. Although this is only the first step in building an integrated process, it is a critical one because awareness leads to collaboration; and collaboration leads to cooperation, and that's what leads to success!

In the words of our field commander, we are saying to our Pentagon, the C crowd, "We are not quite ready to do battle yet. We have some armament (existing products and services), but we may need some artillery support (new products and services) and most likely some troop reinforcements (additional skills or resources)." And by the way, don't forget to shore up the supply chain so that we don't run out of ammunition or food out here on the front lines (capacity enhancements). The fundamental rules of engagement suggest that any force can defeat any other force if it can define the battle. It is now time for us to begin defining our battle plan.

Phase 2 Deliverables

We need to declare our business definition and our place in the industry. Our words will reflect that we can address the opportunities identified in phase 1 by focusing our capabilities and addressing any capacity limitations we may have discovered.

Sources of information:

- Our owners, planners, senior management, and investors
- The data collected in phase 1 that confirmed our market opportunity

We need to list all of the functional activities we will have to provide in order to support our new business plans. This is an important exercise because we will be determining how we are going to add or acquire these functions later on in phase 5 of the program.

Sources of information:

- Competitor's organization charts
- Industry and trade publications
- Financial analyst reports
- Consultants and prior business experience

We will need to list the skills and capabilities we discovered during our internal analysis of our existing organization. We will be comparing this list to the one we just generated to isolate the additional skills needed to execute our plans.

Source of information:

- The internal analysis we just completed

We will need to meet with other members of our management team to inform them of the direction we are planning to take and the required support we are counting on them to provide.

Sources of information:

- The market position we identified in phase 1 that we want to obtain
- The business definition and industry position identified in phase 2
- The skills and functional requirements we identified in phase 2

We are going to document our current sales and distribution channel relationships and estimate their capacity to handle our new requirements. We will also be sure to recognize any potential geographic limitations.

Sources of information:

- The inventory of channels conducted in phase 2
- Prior experience with existing channels

We are going to continue the population of the mother of all matrices which has now become our market planning tool. If we have an established product line, we will have populated the first vertical column with an inventory of our current offerings. If we are a new organization, then we will want to list any product ideas that we are considering.

Sources of information:

- Existing product plans for established organizations
- Existing product development plans
- Product concepts being considered for development

Our goal for phase 2 of the program was to understand our organization's current capabilities and capacity to handle the new challenge we have just been given. We should now have a feel for what we can do with our existing products, resources and alliances, and a better understanding of what we may have to do differently. Knowing what we have to work with, and how we could strengthen this capability, is the second step in developing our plans and organizing our efforts.

Checklist

- We have a definition for our business and our place in the industry.
- We have identified our functional and skill requirements.
- We have inventoried our current capacity for expansion.
- We have inventoried and evaluated our current channels.
- We have catalogued our current and planned product offerings.
- We have begun construction of the mother of all matrices template.

Identification of Customer Set

A Targeted Customer is a single, identifiable, economic buyer for our offer, readily accessible to the sales channel we intend to use, and sufficiently well funded to pay the price for the whole product.

—Geoffrey Moore, Crossing the Chasm

As we enter phase 3 of the program, we begin approaching the areas where we, as marketing professionals, are going to exert the greatest amount of influence. We earlier underscored the need for somebody to have a need to buy something from someone or there was no business. In these next two segments of the program, we are going to define who that somebody is and what that somebody is going to buy. We are also are going to add a few additional caveats to Mr. Moore's excellent definition of a targeted customer. For us, a targeted customer is defined as "one that has a need or desire to buy our offer, the ability to pay for it, and is going to make a purchasing decision within our budgeted time frame." (We call that $Bill's definition.)

We will start segmenting the market at the macro level of the economy and divide our buyers into the three major markets; we need to consider the consumer market, the industrial market, and the government markets. We want to be as specific as we can be in identifying who our targeted customers are, where they are, and why we chose them. This section of our plan needs to consider the following:

- The market segments we identify as suitable segments to pursue (should complement the planner's assessment).

- A recognition of their common buying characteristics and buying behaviors, justifying our groupings of these targeted customers.
- We will want to consider the targeted number of potential customers and their geographic locales.
- We will estimate the total amount of dollars that each of these targeted customer groups spend on products or services like ours, and the percentage or share of that expenditure we are seeking to acquire
- Most importantly, we will need to continue the population of our mother of all matrices and add to it the identified targeted market segments for evaluation

In phase 1 of our program, we suggested that our strategic planners (or our owners) have helped us to identify the markets and industry that our companies operate in. They also highlighted the segments of these markets where they believe our organization has the best opportunities to compete. We now have to find enough potential customers within these identified segments for us to double our market position over the course of the five-year planning period. So who are the target customers within each of these market segments? Where are they located? How do we find them and communicate with them? What are their buying characteristics? How do they make their buying decisions, and, how can we get their attention and influence their buying decision?

Consumer Markets

Let's start with the consumer market because 70 percent of our gross domestic product is driven from personal consumption expenditures. For the consumer market, we will want to know the demographics, psychographics, age groupings, economic status, social groupings, and cultural preferences for our targeted segments. Consumers buy durable goods (houses, automobiles, appliances, etc.), nondurable or consumable goods (food, clothing, personal hygiene products, etc.), and services (carpet cleaning, car washes, landscaping maintenance, etc.). So for us to begin understanding the consumer marketplace, we need to begin by understanding the different kinds of needs consumers are trying to satisfy.

The first approach to understanding consumer needs is to revert to fundamental human needs, the ones that Mr. Maslow identified for us. We have physiological needs (food, clothing, water), we have safety needs (security and protection), we have emotional needs (affection and belonging), we have esteem needs (self-respect and achievement), and we have a desire for fulfillment. Virtually all products and services can be mapped into this hierarchy, and we should start by understanding which of these hierarchical needs our products and services fulfill.

Lifestyle is the second element we will need to understand about our targeted consumer. Even though we are all unique individuals, many of us have adopted similar lifestyles, and these lifestyles embody common behaviors. This is a segmentation technique known as consumer psychographics, and it provides another methodology to understand our market. If we can determine which lifestyle grouping of the consumer population is most likely to acquire our products or services, then we can position and promote our products deliberately to this group. Understanding these behaviors can also provide us with some insight as to how we might be able to influence that particular group's buying decisions. When we add this element to demographics, age, economics, and social groupings, we are able to focus our sales approach on a particular segment of the consumer population.

Eight Male Psychographic Segments

Category	Group I Quiet Man	Group II Traditional Man	Group III Discontent Man	Group IV Ethical Highbrow	Group V Pleasure Seeker	Group VI The Achiever	Group VII The He-Man	Group VIII Sophisticate Man
Physcologic Profile	Family man Self sufficient Shy	Proper & Respectable Secure	Dissatisfied Dreamer Distrustful	Content Cultured Interested in Reforms	Self Centered Emphasizes Masculinity	Hard Working Dedicated Stylish	Gregarious Excitement Dramatic	Intelligent Social Leader
Demographic Profile	Lower Education Lower Economics	Lower Education Middle Economics	Lower Education Lower Economics	Well Educated Mid – upper Economics	Lower Education Lower Economics	Good Education Higher Economics	Well Educated Middle Economics	Best Educated Highest Economics
Consumer Profile	Practical	Conservative	Price Conscious	Interested In Quality	Impulsive Buyer	Status Conscious	Buys for Self Expression	Fashion Conscious
Age Demographic	Older	Oldest	Older	Middle-aged	Middle-aged Or younger	Younger	Youngest	Younger or Middle-aged
Drink Beer	45%	56%	57%	51%	75%	59%	80%	72%

The third thing we need to do is recognize that in satisfying each of these different needs is that human beings tend to cluster into different economic and social strata groupings. As the gossipers say, "Birds of a feather flock together," and we as consumers certainly do. These consumer groupings will gather into common geographic locales as well (communities), and this is where the demographic information provided by the Census Bureau comes into the picture. The census data can help us to geographically locate where these communities are, and we want to be where our targeted lifestyle profile and our targeted demographics meet.

We will also want to understand what the buying behaviors are for each of our targeted consumer segments. A buying behavior is the pattern by which a group of customers acquires products and services. As consumers, we have a tendency to acquire different kinds of durable goods at different stages of our life. For example, we buy homes when we are starting our families and all of the contents for those homes shortly thereafter. We purchase consumable goods all of the time because these items are not sustainable (food, clothing, etc.), and they need to be replenished regularly. We buy services based on a recognizable need for the service—our car may be dirty, or the rugs need to be cleaned.

It would also be worthwhile to know what the buying characteristics of each targeted consumer segment are. A buying characteristic is the process by which a customer solicits and evaluates a purchasing decision. Consumers buying durable goods will usually conduct some degree of research or comparison before making a decision. They often solicit opinions from others in this process and may rely on published information for their basis of comparison. In purchasing consumable goods, consumers usually buy at a point of sale and will be influenced by the convenience of the actual buying experience. For services, consumers tend to rely on word of mouth referrals and are swayed by the opinions and the experiences of others.

The actual decision process is different in each of these different market areas as well. For durable goods, the buying decision is commonly a joint one, and more than one member of the household will weigh in on the process. For consumable products, the actual buyer may not be the ultimate user of the product, and the user requesting the purchase may have been influenced by advertising or by some other point of reference. For services, the individual with the actual need will normally be the one who decides, and he or she will be influenced by the perceived quality received and reasonableness of the price. Sure, these differences are somewhat over simplified, but you can see why they are important to recognize.

So how do we find our targeted customers hiding within all of this consumer market camouflage? We accomplish this by breaking down each of these market segments to a level where we can group similar needs, characteristics, and behaviors into identifiable customer sets. This is an extremely important exercise, because we are going to be making product and channel decisions based on what we learn from this effort. We need to identify a sufficient quantity of these customers with enough combined purchasing power to enable us to reach our planned revenue objectives within our budgeted time frame. Once we understand who these potential customers are, we can then locate where they reside and build plans to reach them.

Our actual selection process will be dependent on our product and service offerings, and which groupings or market segments we believe benefit from their use. If we determine that our product family is best suited for adult males—who are dedicated, hardworking, style conscious, well educated, and highly paid—we can now go looking for them. Our product may then need to be conveniently available within a stylish shopping mall close to the neighborhoods where these gentlemen live. Our product advertising and promotion is going to be directed at the ultimate purchasing consumer, the male profile we just identified. But our target channel, the one we will try to sell to, will most likely be the upscale retail outlet that it is located in those psychographically selected shopping malls, in those demographically suitable suburbs.

This is a very important point, because when we begin to assign sales channels and allocate the resources to support them, we want to make sure that we are spending our resources in an effective manner. We will want to influence the consumer's ultimate purchasing choice, so our product advertising and promotion will be targeted to that end. But the channel we will select to deliver and support our product has to be in the demographic and geographic markets where these targeted consumers shop and reside. We will want to be very selective in making these choices and be very deliberate in terms of how we will market ourselves to that channel.

The example that I like to use as a success model to prove the value of this effort is actually a small women's clothing business located in south Denver, Colorado. This store offers a line of clothing that my wife and her friends refer to as something different, and its clothing line appeals to professional woman. The store originated in a neighborhood closer to the city, but soon found itself competing with a newly constructed upscale shopping mall that attracted the larger and well-known department stores. As a small business, she was unable to afford the rents that the new mall requested; and competing head to head with these larger outlets would be difficult to say the least. The proprietor of this store knew her customers, knew what they wanted, and had a great sense for fashion. But in retail, it's location, location, location.

She learned about a neighborhood just south of town that was beginning to get a lot of renovation attention. It surrounded a beautiful park and was attracting a large number of young upwardly mobile professional couples (her customers). The neighborhood had one commercial street that at one time housed broken-down shops, but was now becoming populated with restaurants, bike shops, and small art galleries. Her targeted customers were living, not just working, in this neighborhood. She moved her store that sells something *different* onto this neighborhood's one commercial street and has been very successful there for the last ten years. As a matter of fact, she now owns the building where her store resides. This story isn't going to make the front page of the *Wall Street Journal*, but it does prove the value of targeting one's customers and finding the best way to reach them.

Industrial Markets

For the industrial markets, we will want to know the different industry classifications, geographic locations, and functions or departments that will ultimately use our products. The very nature of demand in this market is more rigorous and sophisticated than the consumer market because of the complications imbedded within the typical industrial buying process. It can include such things as formal evaluations and technical trials before any purchasing decisions are made. The industrial market also has elements that go beyond just the purchasing process, as the buyer may be acquiring our product or service to support fifty or more of their user markets. This market also has a different economic structure, depending on where the buyer sits in the market chain; and there are different expectations for quality, quantity, and price.

Selecting targeted customers within the industrial markets has to be a very deliberate process. A large account can consume our capacity, and before we know it, the supplier/user roles can be reversed. We are no longer marketing to them, but rather producing exclusively for them, and the economics can change dramatically under this type of scenario. It is best to balance our client base across multiple users that are geographically clustered so that our fulfillment economics can remain competitive. Many of these industrial clients with similar needs tend to cluster in areas where the economic and regulatory considerations are favorable to their business. This is where we want to be.

As we begin to look for targets within this market, we need to be cognizant of a variety of influences that are not always obvious. There are other degrees of rivalry hidden within this market space that can be the real determinants of competition. In addition to the rivalry among known competitors, there is the potential for new entrants and the introduction of substitute products. Existing suppliers could also change their behaviors to become direct providers of parts and services. All of these factors can and do influence industrial buying decisions. So, as we begin the process of identifying our potential target customers, we have to understand where we fit within this set of complex dynamics.

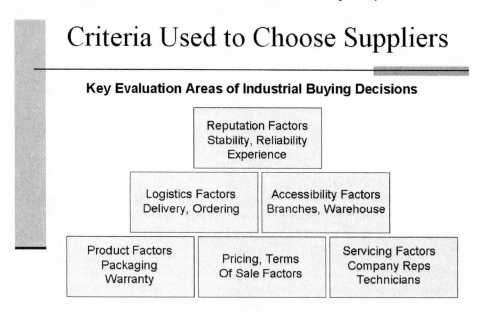

Criteria Used to Choose Suppliers

Key Evaluation Areas of Industrial Buying Decisions

Reputation Factors
Stability, Reliability
Experience

Logistics Factors
Delivery, Ordering

Accessibility Factors
Branches, Warehouse

Product Factors
Packaging
Warranty

Pricing, Terms
Of Sale Factors

Servicing Factors
Company Reps
Technicians

Industrial customers will be utilizing our products or service as a component part of their eventual product or service offering, so we will play a significant role within their value chain. It is absolutely critical that we know how we fit into this model, because this is going to be the qualifier for us, and we need to recognize the value we provide. If we will be trying to substitute or replace someone else's product within their already established value chain, then we are going to need to understand what costs they will encounter in switching products and how we are going to offset these costs. If we are going to be offering a replacement technology, then we need to understand how this would impact their current product offerings.

There are some common purchasing characteristics for us to become familiar with for the industrial segment. In considering the purchase of any product, they will want to understand its compatibility with others that they currently utilize. They will be very aware of the industry's acceptance to making a change from what they are presently using versus our product. If their other supplier's products would not be compatible with our product offering, then it would difficult or impossible for them to consider us. They will also be looking at our company's ability to supply and support our offerings, and this too will become a consideration in their purchasing decision. Traditionally, to replace someone else, we will have to offer a price advantage, a technology advantage, or a new and creative way for the customer to acquire our component.

We also need to know how these targeted industrial customers will eventually make their buying decision. Unlike the consumer market, there can be any number of influences engaged in making the eventual buying choice for an industrial product. The purchase may be contracted through the purchasing department, but it's the division operations manager who will actually make the selection. He or she won't make that determination without support from other operating managers and engineers, because the choice has to fit into their existing activities and plans as well. All of this is also subject to the availability of funding, so finance and accounting may also get into the act. As we pick our target customers in this industrial segment, we need to recognize and respect the complexity of this buying process.

Example of Purchasing Influences

Buying Company Personnel	Primary Area of Interest	Secondary Area of Interest	Specifications	Preliminary Budget Approval	Competitive Bidders List	Equipment Or Vendor Evaluation	Equipment Or Vendor Selection
Purchasing Department	Initial Cost Reliability Reputation	Operating Cost & Savings			X	X	X
Operating Manager	Operating Cost Reliability	Initial Cost Technology Savings	X			X	
Engineering	Operating Costs Maintenance	Reliability Field Proven Vendor	X		X	X	
Financial Department	Initial Cost Life Cycle ROI	Vendor Reputation Terms		X			X
Division or General Manager	Reliability Life Cycle Costs	Potential Savings		X			X
Corporate Management	Technology Reliability Life Cycle	Vendor Experience		X			X

This is going to require us to take an additional step in assembling our information about this group. We are going to have to identify what positions within these companies are the traditional influencers and who are the individuals that occupy those positions. Remember, as part of our targeting process we are trying to determine where we fit into their plans, not just where they fit into ours. So taking the time to understand their criteria for supplier selection and who influences that selection will help us to weed out those prospects that have no reason to consider us at all. If we do not fit into their value chain, then they are not a prospect for our consideration, no matter how big they are.

We are going to want this additional level of detail, so we will consider using an even more detailed data source to acquire it such as Hoover's (www. hoovers.com) or ZoomInfo USA (www.zoominfo.com). From these sources, we can obtain the names and positions of the individuals within these firms whom we may need to contact. For smaller organizations that do not have access to these database resources, a great deal of information can be gleaned from industry or trade publications and then validated via the Internet. Taking the time to research these potential customers, before investing in a sales effort, will help our organization to "down select" to the prospects that provide us with the greatest opportunity.

The last important factor to be aware of in the industrial segment is the sensitivity that industrial buyers have about their proprietary processes and information. When we begin discussing our place at the table with an established enterprise, we will most often be placed under nondisclosure. A large industrial buyer will not openly share information and will want reassurance that if they do share information with us that it will not leak out into the market where their competitors can gain access to it. They may also request "favored-nation pricing" as assurance that we will not give these same competitors any sort of a price advantage over them if they should choose to purchase our products.

Once again, the actual targeting decisions will be dependent on the kinds of products and services we provide. Selecting a market or industry segment is the first step in identifying potential buyers, but the next step is the most critical. None of us are going to be successful with every potential client all the time, so we need to make sure that we have identified a large enough universe of potential buyers to allow for this variable. If we need to acquire five new accounts of a certain size, then we better identify at least ten and maybe even fifteen to be safe. Our acid test will be to estimate the amount of product or service this universe of targeted customers currently buys and then take a reasonable penetration rate of that number to estimate our potential. If the revenue opportunity does not enable us to reach our assigned growth objective, then we need to find additional prospects.

In my last corporate assignment, I was responsible for the North American operations of an engineering and construction company that designs and builds commercial infrastructure. The division I worked in supported the communications industry and had enjoyed a great deal of success during the heydays of building fiber optic networks and revamping cable distribution systems. When the industry experienced a downturn in 1999-2000, the firm found itself in the uncomfortable position of having to downsize. Needless to say, this was a frustrating period for the managers and employees of this operating division.

I was challenged to restart the marketing effort for this business segment and quickly recognized that the relationships the firm had established in the past several years were limited to terrestrial carriers, a segment of the industry that was no longer expanding. The larger firms in this segment had already completed their major capital programs, and these clients no longer had a need to add additional capacity. Although the terrestrial communication companies were no longer digging up the streets, wireless communication carriers were rapidly expanding and building their infrastructures. This growth segment of the industry was going gangbusters, and the competition between the participants to get their facilities built and their new services marketed provided plenty of opportunity for us.

We refocused our efforts to support this growing segment of the industry and adjusted our internal support structures to accommodate these new requirements. The result was a rather dramatic turnaround, accomplished within a short period of three years. Targeting this new group of customers has led to a whole new set of relationships that continue to provide opportunity for this company. We focused our efforts on a set of targeted customers that we identified, and then tailored our value proposition specifically to their issues. This was accomplished by segmenting the market (wireless vs. wireline), targeting our customers (selecting who we were going to call on), and focusing our resources to serve this identified need. The results speak for themselves, a 1,500 percent increase in revenues within a three-year period.

Government Markets

For the government markets, we will want to know what agencies will be spending money for our kind of services and what programs they are considering that we could participate in. In some respects, it is easier to determine where government-buying influences are because they publish their intentions and conduct business in an open and competitive manner. On the other hand, it can be difficult to succeed in this environment because all of our competitors can gain access to the same information we can. We all compete for the same contracts, and we all may have to disclose some of our cost and pricing information as part of the process. What makes these opportunities worth pursuing is the incredible size of the market. It is measured in the trillions of dollars, and the value and duration of the contracts that are awarded can make the effort very worthwhile.

Segmenting the federal market is a relatively easy process because a great deal of information about its commercial activities is reflected in their published budget available from the Office of Management and Budget. The OMB provides an accounting for all the planned expenditures for each government agency, as well as reconciliations by expense categories. So, if we want to know how much money the federal government is going to spend on information technology for example, we can look it up. If we want to know which agencies are going to spend the most money on information technology programs over the next five years, we can look that up as well. It's just that there are a lot of agencies, subagencies, and sub-subagencies to look up.

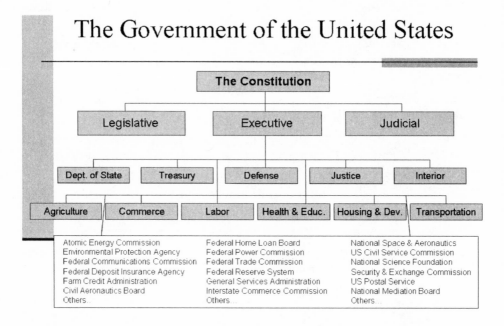

The federal government does have, just like the consumer and industrial markets, some buying characteristics that provide us with insight into its purchasing decision processes. For example, for its administrative requirements the federal government will seek to leverage its buying power and seek the best economic alternatives. For its information system and technology requirements, it will be relying more on the technical and program management skills of its eventual supplier, so it will consider this in its decision process. Since these elements will be more highly valued in its selection process, our proposal should emphasize these capabilities. For its defense and intelligence needs, the federal government will be seeking leading edge technology companies with specialized experience in these sensitive areas.

Once we have identified the expense categories we are interested in and located the agencies we want to target (the ones spending the money), we can now start looking for suitable programs. Each of the federal agencies publishes a forecast of planned activities and programs, and sets a schedule of events to communicate these requirements to industry. They will traditionally hold conferences to communicate the attributes of their program requirements and encourage industry to work together to help meet them. If we can qualify our company through this competitive solicitation process, then we should be able to offer our products or services to the government.

The federal government also provides other sources to help businesses discover new opportunities within its ranks. Federal Business Opportunities (www.fedbizops.com) provides access to all of the existing and pending solicitations the federal government is procuring. This notice service, formerly the *Commerce Business Daily*, features an electronic search capability that can help us to find the specific kinds of programs that we may be looking for. In addition, we can sort through their entire database by federal agency, by procurement category, or by special procurement considerations (like small business set-asides), as well as general categories of services. If it is out there, you can find it through the FedBizOps search engine and learn who the program manager is and the office that will eventually be awarding the contract.

Federal Programs & Opportunities

COMMERCE BUSINESS DAILY

A daily list of U.S. Government procurement invitations, contract awards, subcontracting leads, sales of surplus property and foreign business opportunities.

Login to begin searching the FBO/CBD

Search the FBO Here =>

Home Page

CBD/FBO Online

CBD/FBO Email

About Us

Contact Us

Privacy

Categories

No. Notes

Archives

Search

Help

Login

Register

Search the notices in the FedBizOpps (FBO), formerly the Commerce Business Daily(CBD), for federal procurement bidding opportunities, contracts awarded, special notices and surplus government sales. You can search using keywords or phrases relevant to your business or select from over 100 business categories using NEPAC's powerful FBO Online search engine service.

If you need to zero in on the announcements in the FBO/CBD that are relevant to your business on a daily basis, then our FBO Email service is perfect for you. By selecting keywords and categories we'll then use our powerful database software to filter the hundreds of daily announcements that pertain to your business and deliver them to you every day via email in a full, easy-to-read format.

Service note: Effective January 1, 2002, the FedBizOpps (FBO) database (CBD) has replaced the Commerce Business Daily (CBD). This new FBO/CBD database is identical to the old CBD format. NEPAC has successfully completed this transition and will continue to service our clients with the most up-to-date and comprehensive federal procurement information available. For more information call: 800-932-7761 or email us at: online@cbdweb.com

State and local governments have similar buying characteristics, but their behavior is not as formally structured as the federal government. They too publish annual budgets and openly disclose their proposed spending and expense allocations. They will usually have a requirement for open competition, but the individual state or local government's selection criteria may consider other influences, such as local business interests and regional economic impacts in their selection process. Selecting the state or local government agency that will use our products, understanding how and where our products and services are best applied, is the right approach.

So, the right methodology for segmenting the government markets is to acquire a copy of their published budget and identify the agencies that have the funding to purchase our products and services. Next contact those agencies to obtain copies of their forecasted activities and planned programs. Identify the programs that our products and services would be valued in and then make sure we are listed with the federal CCR (Central Contractor Registration) or with the individual state or local government we are pursuing. We will want to attend all the program prequalification meetings and all the vendor information days for the programs we have an interest in competing for. If we are going to participate in these government markets, we have to be prepared to invest time in a decision cycle that can be very long and often unpredictable.

At the time of this writing, I am helping an emerging technology company called Adventos LLC (www.adventos.com), expand its business into the federal government market space. When I first spoke with the principles about this effort, they immediately wanted to duplicate their commercial practices and start hiring sales representatives to go call on local federal government agency offices. I suggested that they postpone that thought and take the time to understand what their target market is and which agencies would have the highest probable use for their service offerings. They also needed to get a few other bureaucratic obstacles out of the way (such as becoming listed on the Central Contractor's Register) so that these agencies could actually buy their services.

Adventos LLC does an excellent job of providing technical training, and technical skills are required to be refreshed within the government's information technology community. After guiding their firm through the government registration process, obtaining pricing schedule approvals and so forth, we set about targeting the potential users for their services. We selected the CIO (Chief Information Officer) community within the federal agencies that have the highest propensity to utilize technology. Our assumption was that if the agency processed enormous amounts of information, they had a need for a large staff of Information Technology professionals. Information Technology professionals need to stay current on the technology they use, and therefore need continual technical training.

The results are just beginning to come in, but we are already starting to see the benefits of this focus. Had Adventos just gone out and hired sales people, they would not have accomplished much more than spending money. The current alternative, which was accomplished for a minimal amount of investment, has now provided the critical information about their company's services directly to the user community that can benefit most from acquiring them. Their service offering is now positioned as a training option for the professional development of government IT professionals, a good place to be.

By taking the time to understand who their targeted customers are, where they are, and how to reach them, Adventos has improved its chances for success ten fold. They are going to follow up this initial program with a series of new capability updates and expect to garner their fair share of the new fiscal years technical training dollars. They have now targeted their marketing tactics and are spending their efforts and resources where it matters. The return from this investment can be extraordinary!

From our segmentation efforts, we should now know who our targeted customers are, how many there are, where they are, how they buy, why they buy, and what we need to do to influence that buying decision. This is important information to have because in the next segment of our program, we will be matching our products and services to these customer groups, and we will want to know which offerings are attractive to which targets. We are also going to be exploring different channels to reach and support these same-targeted customers. The database we are developing as a result of this effort should now become company sensitive information, as it will be the basis for our product plans, our channel plans, and our commercial relationships in these identified markets.

One additional step we may choose to take at this juncture would be to begin the construction of our customer database. We are conducting a considerable amount of research to discover what we want to know about these targeted customer groups, so establishing a repository for this information would save us an additional step in the future. Ultimately, we are going to want to track our actual sales results to the assumptions we are making about these groups, so collecting and cataloguing this information into a database that we can access later would be beneficial to our efforts going forward. Having this database will also help us with our channel management programs and territory assignments.

Back to the Matrix

One of the difficult challenges of assembling our list of target customers and identified market segments is quantifying the value of their purchasing power for our products. We can only estimate this number, but we calculate our estimates from some reasonable rules of logic. If our targeted customers are in the consumer segment, then the dollars these consumers would have to spend could possibly come from their disposable income. We can determine what that dollar figure is from the published census data. We will then take a reasonable percentage of these dollars as an estimate for the amount they would have to spend on our products. For industrial clients, we can look at what the value of the products we are attempting to substitute is within our targeted group, and then calculate some reasonable penetration rate. For government programs, we should assume a reasonable win percentage of the total programs we are targeting to pursue, and then calculate the value of what we intend to provide.

It is time for us to return to our mother of all matrices and populate the information we have just learned. We need to represent it in a manner that will allow us to add these new variables in a way that will support our evaluation process. In other words, for an identified consumer profile, how many of them are there out there and how much will this customer segment spend for our kinds of products or services in the aggregate? So at the top of our vertical columns we have to estimate what the aggregate purchasing power of this group is worth. We need to have enough market opportunity to meet our objectives. If we are going to double our market share from 10 to 20 percent by progressively growing revenues at 27 percent per annum, we may need a lot of customers.

We are going to formally recognize each of these market segments we have just selected as a new vertical column, and then create a subtotal field that represents the estimated purchasing power for each of them. This estimate is important as we are going to be estimating the potential revenue impact that each of these targeted customer groups could have on our future plans. As we establish and populate each of these new fields, we will begin to discover possible targets of opportunity for us to explore, as there will be spaces within our matrix where we do not currently have current activities planned. Displaying this matrix as a visual aide will help us to discover these areas and work through this process.

"Mother of All Matrices"

Market Segments		Consumer Market Targets Potential Value $ "X"			Industrial Market Targets Potential Value $ "Y"		
Product Groupings	Current Plans	Segment A $	Segment B $	Segment C $	Segment D $	Segment E $	Segment F $
Product A	Heavily Promote						
Product B	Increase Distribution						
Product C	Increase Distribution						
Product D	Improve Packaging						
Summary							
Product E	Exit Market						
Product F	Exit Market						
Product G	Exit Market						
Summary							

Now that we have populated our mother of all matrices, it is the time to give ourselves the first acid test. When we add up the potential market potential for all of the targets we have just selected, it has to provide enough opportunity for us to achieve our revenue objectives. For example, if we are targeting a 10 percent share in the first year, then 10 percent of the total of our targeted customer's purchases has to enable us to meet this revenue objective. In year two, we may need to achieve 12 percent; year three, 15 percent; and so on. If we have not identified a large enough universe of potential customers, then we need to go back and work at it again. Opportunity is a primary ingredient for our success; and if we haven't identified enough opportunity in our first round, then we need to improve this process in our second attempt.

The complexity of what we are creating will vary from organization to organization, depending on the size and quantity of our business interests. If we are a local or regional enterprise that is focused in only one geographic market, then we may only take up part of the wall. If we are a multinational enterprise, operating in various vertical markets around the globe, then we may take up an entire wall for each geography we have targeted to do business in (e.g., North America, Europe, etc.). At the top of our mother of all matrices along the horizontal axis, we have now added our vertical columns for each of the various markets, market segments, and targeted customer groups we have identified. Over on the left hand side of our matrix, the initial vertical columns we created, is a representation of our existing products and product plans that we developed in phase 2.

The reason we are creating this mother of all matrices will become obvious as we continue throughout our program. In phase 4, we will be mapping our current and future products to each of these targeted customer groups. What will become obvious as a result of this effort is the discovery of areas within our matrix that are empty. Intersections where we will not have enough identified channels or areas where we may have totally underserved potential. There could be areas where we currently do not have products and services to offer, and other areas where we could provide new products or services. These will become our targets of opportunity for us to take advantage of. The targets that provide the greatest value for the investments we would need to make are the ones we are going to consider.

As we get ready to move from phase 3 to phase 4 of the program, we could find ourselves in a large conference room that has a big table in the middle. There should now be three piles of information on the table; one that contains information about our business climate and environment; a second that summarizes our business focus, core competency, and current capacity; and a third that contains information about the markets, market segments, and potential customers we have identified as targets. On the wall is hanging (or projected) our mother of all matrices which has been populated with a vertical column of our current product offerings and their attributes. We have now added to this matrix a series of new vertical columns that contain the identity of each our targeted market segments and the potential purchasing power they possess.

As we return to our metaphorical battlefield, we find ourselves beginning to define the battle plan. As field commanders, we are surveying our targets (the customers we are going to pursue) and where we will be pursuing them. We now need to match our armament (our products and services) to these targets and determine the best means (channels) to get them there.

Phase 3 Deliverables

We need to declare the customer profiles we have selected as the target for our products and services. We should be able to quantify what percentage of the general population they represent, their purchasing power, their buying characteristics, and the geographies where they reside.

Sources of information:

- US Census Bureau demographics
- Market research sources
- Consumer psychographic profiles
- Prior experience
- Consumer data bases (e.g. Claritas' Prizm)

We need to declare the industrial market segments we are going to pursue, their industry characteristics and potential value. We have selected this group of targets because they have an identified problem set or need that we feel we can fulfill with our offerings.

Sources of information:

- Industry lists—*Fortune, Forbes, Business Week*, etc.
- Industry segment listings—Lead 411, Business Miner
- Trade publications and published surveys
- Contracted market research
- Commercially available market research

We need to further segment this list by industry classification and identify the industries that have the highest probability to use our offering.

Sources of information:

- US Department of Commerce, NAICS codes
- Dun & Bradstreet, SIC
- Industry lists—*Fortune, Forbes, Business Week*, etc.
- Industry segment listings—Lead 411, Business Miner

We will next segment this list to a more granular level by selecting those specific companies that appear to be the best prospects for our offerings. We will be deliberate enough to have selected a large-enough target list to ensure that we are able to solicit a sufficient volume of transaction to satisfy our plan requirements.

Sources of information:

- Industry segments listings—Lead 411, Business Miner, Hoovers
- Trade publications and published surveys
- Commercially available market research
- Prior actual experience with similar offerings

For our government markets, we will want to identify the specific government agencies we are targeting, the budgeted amount they will be spending in an expense category that matches our interests, and the identification of new programs that we are interested in pursuing.

Sources of information:

- US Government Office of Management and Budget
- FedBizOps database
- Targeted agencies Web sites and published materials

We will next begin to assemble (or add to) our customer database. This information will also be used in the next segment of the program to help select the appropriate channels to serve these customers.

Sources of information:

- US Census Bureau demographics
- Hoover's D&B listings
- InfoUSA listings
- Industry publications and listings
- Office of Management and Budget
- FedBizOps database
- The Internet, directly from Web sites

We will populate our mother of all matrices with the additional vertical columns for each of the market classifications we have selected. At the top of the column we will identify the segment, the number of potential targeted customers we have selected, and the potential purchasing power of that group for our products and services.

Sources of information:

> Estimates of expenditures for similar products or services
> Mathematical calculations based on estimates of units and sales prices
> Commercially available market research
> Trade publications and published surveys
> Prior actual experience with similar offerings

Last and not least, we will want to *plot* the geography of the targeted accounts we have selected. If we are shipping hardware, then inbound and outbound logistics can be a sizable operating cost to deal with, so being geographically positioned to minimize these costs is smart business.

Sources of information:

> Hoover's D&B listings
> InfoUSA listings
> Targeted customer Web sites
> Census Bureau demographics
> Government agency Web sites

Our goal for phase 3 was to discover enough existing or new targeted customers to enable us to meet the new challenges we have been given. Knowing who our potential customers are and where they are is the third step in developing our plans and organizing our efforts.

Phase 3 Checklist

> We have identified our targeted market segments (consumer).
> We have identified our targeted industry classifications (industrial).
> We have identified our targeted government agencies and programs.
> We understand their common purchasing characteristics.
> We have populated our mother of all matrices with their potential.
> We have begun the construction of our customer database.

Determine Product

and Sales Strategy

There are risks and costs to a program of action, but they are far less than the long-range risks and costs of comfortable inaction.

—*John F. Kennedy*

The purpose of phase 4 of our program is to begin matching the right set of products to the right set of targeted customers and then explore different ways to distribute them. Once we know which products and services go where, both our existing products and the new ones we may choose to provide, then we can start channel surfing to pick the best vehicles to reach them. The combinations of different choices we will be considering have to progressively grow our revenues year over year so that we can achieve our new market-share objective. It is in this phase of the program that we begin to marry our organization's strategy (double our market share) to the actual tactics and activities that we must perform to enable this to happen.

Our first step will be to begin the development of the product plan we will need to accomplish our growth objectives. We approach this task by mapping our existing products, the ones we inventoried in phase 2 of the program, with the targeted customer groups we identified in phase 3. What we are trying to discover throughout this process is which set of targeted customers is most likely to buy which set of products and services. What we gain from this exercise is the beginnings of our eventual product plan, the one that when we add it up enables us to achieve our new revenue requirement.

Our second step will be to identify all of the channel options that could enable us to reach these targeted customers and support our products. One of the benefits we gain from building this relationship matrix of ours is that it helps us to quantify both the total value we expect to gain from our product sales, and the total value we plan on benefiting from selling to each of our targeted customers. Collecting and representing this information in this format will help us to recognize other integrated relationships within our marketing mix, such as the allocation of advertising and promotion costs.

The third step in the process will be to calculate the available gross margin that we believe could be generated from each of the different scenarios we are going to consider. We will determine this by adding up the number of product units we think we can sell to each of these targeted groups, multiply it times our expected sales price, then subtract our direct costs to determine our gross margins. We will then subtract our other variable marketing costs from each of these gross margin calculations to determine the contribution (available gross margin) we can expect from expending these marketing efforts.

In this phase of our program, we want to identify our product and sales options. To accomplish this we will need to consider the following:

The product units that we could sell to each of our identified targeted customers and their resulting contribution

Our product pricing and promotion plans, recognizing the value of what it is we are considering to offer

Our product management plans, the tactics we are considering for each of our offerings in relation to their current life cycles

Our new product plans and the choices we are considering to invest in and how they will fit into our new product plans

Our new product investment requirements, the timing and dollars we are seeking to develop new products and fill our product voids

Our channel selection options for each of our target markets and product sets

An estimate of the channel and promotional costs we have available to spend on each of these product and customer groups

The population of our mother of all matrices with our product assumptions mapped to targeted customers for evaluation

Product Planning

Every product or service that we provide exists to meet a need or solve a problem, and they all fit somewhere into our customer's real or perceived value chain. A value chain is the sequence of events that incorporates our product or service into an application performed by the user of our product of service. Different products provide different benefits to different users at different points in time. Understanding how each of our products is used by our targeted customers is an excellent way to understand their potential value to those customers who buy them.

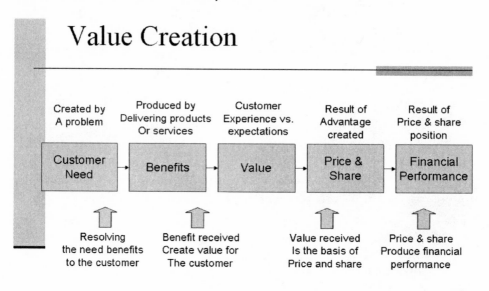

Our approach to developing our product plan is to return to our mother of all matrices and make provisions to accommodate the additional variables we need to consider. We accomplish this by expanding the product fields in our matrix to allow us to vary the number of individual product units we are going to sell. We start by mapping our current product plan (the existing and planned products populated in our first vertical column) to each of these targeted segments and estimate the number of units we intend to sell to each market segment (the targeted customer groups represented by the vertical columns added in phase 3). Where we already have an established relationship, we can forecast this estimate based on our prior experience. Where we do not have a relationship, we can only presume that we could sell some number of our current products to this identified group.

We can now calculate the amount of revenues that will be generated from these unit sales (unit price X units sold), the direct costs (unit cost X units sold), and the resulting gross margins they will contribute. We are quantifying the actual value of selling a known number of existing products to the targeted customers within the various market segments we are now considering. We accomplish this by simply mapping each of our current product offerings to each set of targeted customer groups and then calculate what our resulting revenues could be. This initial calculation will be our starting point, an estimate of the revenues we could produce in our first year with our existing product plans.

Our mother of all matrices has now become populated with our targeted market segments (the horizontal axis across the top identifying each targeted segment) and our existing product offerings (the vertical axis groupings of each of our products, their life cycle stages, and current economics). It is not unusual for the same products to have different price points in different market segments, so in the expansion of our matrix we need to be sure to allow for this possibility.

We will next add the capability to total the values of what we have populated by adding up both the value of the expected product sales (horizontally totaled) and the total sales within a market segment (vertically totaled).

We are going to create way out at the end of our matrix additional columns for each of the calendar years within our planning horizon. We will have to be able to calculate how much revenue and contribution each of the different scenarios we are going to consider will generate within different time horizons. We are creating this dynamic environment within our mother of all matrices so that we can evaluate different scenarios for different years of our product planning. Products with maturing life cycles will generate lesser revenues in later years, products in earlier life cycle stages could generate more in later years. We need to be able to change and substitute these different variables as part of our process.

When we push the total buttons, we will be able to see how much each product group is currently worth across all targeted segments (horizontal totals) and how much each market segment can generate from our existing product sales (vertical totals). There will most likely be a number of intersections where we are either do not currently offer a product to an identified set of potential customers, or where we currently don't have a replacement product that matches an existing customer group. As we said earlier, discovering these voids is a good thing, and for every void we discover we also discover a target of opportunity for us to consider.

"Mother of All Matrices"

Market Segments	Consumer Market Target Potential Value Segment A $100M								
Product Groupings	Current Plans	Units	Unit Price	Total Revenues	Unit Cost	Total Cost	Unit Margin	Total Margin	Year #1 Totals
Product A	Heavily Promote	1,000	$250	$250,000	$175	$175,000	$75	$75,000	
Product B	Increase Distribution	3,000	$500	$1,500,000	$400	$1,200,000	$100	$300,000	
Product C	Increase Distribution	2500	$400	$1,000,000	$300	$750,000	$100	$250,000	
Product D	Improve Packaging	500	$100	$50,000	$60	$30,000	$40	$20,000	
Summary Group. A		7,000		$2,800,000		$2,155,000		$645,000	xxxxxx
Product E	Exit Market	100	$200	$20,000	$210	$21,000	$-10	$-1,000	
Product F	Exit Market	75	$100	$7,500	$100	$7,500	$0	$0	
Product G	Exit Market	50	$50	$2,500	$60	$3,000	$-10	$-500	
Summary Group. B		225		$30,000		$31,500		$-1,500	xxxxxx

We want to highlight these gaps in our matrix because this is where the opportunities will be. Even though the current populated totals may satisfy our first year's revenue requirement, it will most likely not satisfy our requirements in future years. Our mother of all matrices will become the tool that we will use to consider and evaluate all of our possible alternatives. If we choose to add additional product units for sale to existing customers, we could potentially grow revenues. If we chose to enter new market segments with existing products, we could also instigate new revenue growth. Should we elect to enter new market segments with new products, we can then grow revenues even more. We need to be able to explore all of these options and then select the ones that provide us with the best opportunities.

Our mother of all matrices has to allow for the calculation of any number of different combinations at different snapshots in time. We are going to generate more than one set of alternatives as our product plan evolves. We will be constructing different combinations of products and customers to support each year of our five-year planning horizon. We do not have to be specific at this point in our data collection and evaluation, but eventually we will have to determine what products and in what quantities we are going to provide for what customers in what time frames. Our goal right now is to discover whether or not we have sufficient products available in sufficient quantity to achieve the necessary revenues for each calendar year of our aggressive plan.

These initial discoveries will become our planning baseline, our starting point from which we will be developing the alternative choices to consider for moving the organization forward. One issue that may become apparent from this effort is that several of our existing products are in life cycle stages that will not generate the future revenues needed to achieve our goals. The opportunity that accompanies this realization is that we have the option to develop and introduce a replacement product to offset that outcome. There may also be newly discovered market segments or geographies (discovered in phase 3) where we do not currently have a product to provide, and this is another area for potential growth. Everywhere that there is a product gap or a market segment uncovered provides us with a new opportunity to explore.

This is the coordination step between our targeting process (phase 3 of the program) and our product planning process (phase 4). We need to have enough of a market to sell to (the aggregate of the purchasing power of our targeted customer groups) and a comprehensive set of products to provide to them (our arsenal of product and service offerings), or the math just doesn't work. Mapping our existing product plans into the matrix enables us to calculate our business-as-usual scenario, what we will look like if we do nothing different over the course of the next five years. This is where our confidence starts to build, or the inverse, our concerns start to take hold. When we add it all up, we can either meet the C crowd's growth projections, or we will have to augment our product plans until we close the gaps.

As we begin to massage the data and look at the various combinations available to us, we must have the discipline to recognize the impact that these choices could have on other areas of the marketing mix. There are going to be at the very least additional production costs that could either positively or negatively affect the direct unit cost of producing more of these same products. Additionally, if we elect to develop or acquire new products to fill identified gaps, there is going to be additional product introduction costs. In the next segment of the program, where we formally define our objectives and our operating requirements, we will be setting our budgets for these expenditures.

Part of our product planning effort has to be identifying where these risks are, and then adding to our list of current considerations the option to develop or acquire new product offerings. We may have to develop a set of replacement products, or we may not. We may choose to introduce a whole new set of product offerings, or we may not. It will all depend on the outcome of the evaluation process we have now begun, and the impact that these kinds of decisions will have on the outcome of our overall market plan. For our purposes (our hypothetical challenge), we will assume that we have a need to develop some new products.

Product Development

When we pushed our total buttons, we discovered that our existing product plans came up short of meeting the new growth objectives we have been given. Since this is the case, then we will have to introduce something new or different than what we presently provide. This is easier said than done as discovering new product ideas is a very, very difficult process. Every company is constantly looking for new products or services to offer, and applying market based management principles can help with the discovery of these new possibilities. For now, we can only offer the reader a list of places to go look that can help you unearth what these new products might be.

To start, we begin looking within our own organizations and seek ideas from other functional groups. If our company is large enough to have a research and engineering group, this can be a good place to start. Another group to look to is our direct sales organization and other sales channels that are in constant communications with the ultimate customer. Our own marketing staff and contracted market research firms are good sources as well, as they track trends and changes within and across the industry. We can also look to employee suggestions, customer suggestions, inquiries, and complaints. These are excellent sources of feedback on our existing products with respect to features and functionality that can lead to successful product enhancements.

We also need to look externally and speak with others who are visible within the marketplace. Brokers, factory distributors, manufacturers' agents, representatives, wholesalers, and jobbers can all be good sources of changing requirements. We want to stay abreast of what our competitors are currently offering, so we should speak with the customers of our competitors to learn what they may be proposing. We can peruse mail order and trade catalogues, attend exhibits and trade shows, and pay particular attention to new foreign products that are entering the market. And finally, we could contact inventors and patent attorneys seeking business partners, manufacturer's component providers, research universities and laboratories, industrial consultants, industry trade associations, and professional standards and technical associations.

This is a very important step in our product planning process, the recognition of the new products we will have to develop in order to meet the needs of our targeted customers. We now know that in order to meet the year-five revenue requirement of our market plan, we have to find a way to fill these product voids. In order to accomplish this, we must have a process to evaluate and develop these new products and services. This takes us to the next step of our product planning process, establishing a methodology for new product development.

We have to present our recommendations for new product considerations in a way that enables the organization to view them from a company-wide perspective. Since we will be requesting investment capital for this development effort, we will have to interface with a committee of stakeholders that come from different disciplines within our organization. We need to organize our thoughts and ideas in a format that enables this group to understand the nuances and differences among the choices we are proposing. The more clearly we present this information, the easier it will be for this group to decide, and the higher their level of confidence will be in supporting the final selections

We are not going to have all of the answers at this early stage of discovery, but we do have enough information to frame the opportunity these new product concepts represent. We have already identified any disruptive or new technologies in phase 1, we understand our core competency and capability to develop these products from phase II, and we have just identified the potential customers who have a need for these new product ideas in phase 3. We will now provide a list of product concepts for consideration, and as we learn more about them throughout the development process, we will communicate their cost to develop and validate the benefits they can provide.

Product Screening Model

Activity	Weight	Good	Fair	Poor
Technical	15	Requirements Readily Available	Moderate Deficiencies	Major Deficiencies
Operations	25	Requirements Readily Available	Moderate Deficiencies	Major Deficiencies
Marketing	25	Allows Minimal Competition	Allows Moderate Competition	High Barriers to Entry
Profit	20	Exceeds Organizational Objectives	Meets Organizational Objectives	Does NOT Meet Minimum Objectives
Capital Required	15	Exceeds Required ROI	Meets Required ROI	Does NOT Meet Minimum Objectives

Once we decide on these new product ideas, we begin to transform them from concept into actual products. Our initial screening process will require us to ask three fundamental questions: Is this new product opportunity real? With the development of this product, can we (both the company and the product) effectively compete? And finally, are the financial returns going to be there considering the investments we are making? To find the answers to these questions we engage in a process that will systematically govern our new product's development via a series of stage gates. The investments we make at each one of these stages of the development cycle must be in proportion to the opportunity that these new product ideas represent.

This process takes some discipline, and it has to be managed outside of the mainstream of other product management activities. Remember earlier when we identified the different investment choices that we wanted the C crowd to consider funding? Well, we didn't really expect to get all of that money at once, and we need to have a mechanism that sustains their confidence in our development approach to keep the funding faucet turned on. The best way to accomplish this is with a rigidly defined process that takes all of the noise out of the development sequence and validates each stage of our progress.

There are several product development models around to govern this undertaking, and we could easily dedicate a whole separate publication to just that topic. But here is a marketing practitioner's overly simplified model that provides a measurable seven-step approach. It can be readily understood by all of the stakeholders and consists of the following stage gates:

> Stage 1—a definition of the product, its functionality, attributes, and applicability to fill the customer need we have identified (requirements)
>
> Stage 2—a hypothesis with respect to the opportunity it will provide, potential market size, and the customer's willingness to pay (volume and price assumptions)
>
> Stage 3—a formal assessment of the product's potential supported by market research, customer interviews, etc., quantifying its parameters (life cycle revenue potential)
>
> Stage 4—the development of a production plan that considers the technical requirements and manufacturing challenges (project plan)
>
> Stage 5—the actual physical development of the product, its user documentation, and its training and testing requirements (prototype)

Stage 6—technical trials, market trials, and pricing trials to confirm market demand and acceptance (alpha, beta trials, market trials)

Stage 7—controlled product introduction into specific markets to targeted customers with specific promotion (staged introduction)

Product Development

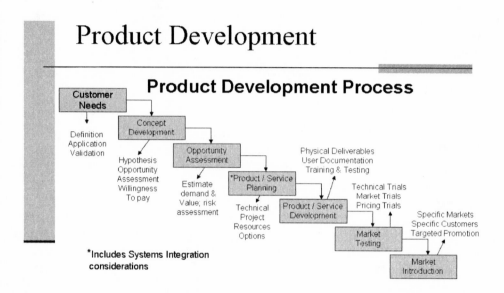

We also advocate that this development process be formalized into a project management model so that every step and activity is tracked with relationship to the critical milestone deliverables and required timelines. If we do not do this, we run the risk of missing the market timing of the opportunity we are trying to capture, not to mention the potential for runaway cost that could occur. We have to be willing to abandon the effort at any one of the critical stages in the process if the data tells us that we are on the wrong track. Most organizations struggle with this, so we must insist on a governance model that tells us where we are on any given effort at any given time in the development cycle.

Estimating the timing, value, and market acceptance of any new product is difficult, and predicting the resulting revenues is always somewhat of a gamble. We are going to have to populate our product plans with a certain number of units and dollars for products that are not yet developed. This will become one of our critical success factors, and it will be highlighted in our measurement systems in phase 6 of our program. If the products do not get through the development cycle and into the market within our budgeted timelines, then the product and revenue plan is at risk. So needless to say, we want to build in a series of safeguards to help mitigate this risk. A little market pressure can be a good incentive to figure this out.

Once we gain a feel for the timing of these new product initiatives, we will go back to our mother of all matrices and populate the product gaps with our estimates for these new offerings. Our development plans may fulfill the identified needs in one market segment, but not necessarily every market segment. We may have to wait for two or three years before some of these products will actually be available, so we need to understand this reality and budget that timing factor accordingly. This does not give us an excuse not to grow the business; it just encourages us to seek other options until we get these new products to market. (Hopefully, this will begin to reinforce the value of going through a program like Targeted Tactics® on an annual basis, as it will enable you to mitigate this timing risk in future years.)

"Mother of All Matrices"

Potential Revenues by Year

Product Groupings	Current Plans	Plan Yr. #1	Plan Yr. #2	Plan Yr. #3	Plan Yr. #4	Plan Yr. #5
Existing Product A	Heavily Promote	$250,000	$275,000	$300,000	$315,000	$325,000
Existing Product B	Increase Distribution	$1,500,000	$1,750,000	$2,000,000	$2,200,000	$2,400,000
Existing Product C	Increase Distribution	$1,000,000	$1,100,000	$1,250,000	$1,500,000	$1,750,000
Existing Product D	Improve Packaging	$50,000	$60,000	$75,000	$100,000	$150,000
Summary		$2,800,000	$3,160,000	$3,625,000	$4,115,000	$4,625,000
New Product E	Heavily Promote	$0	$200,000	$500,000	$750,000	$1,250,000
New Product F	Heavily Promote	$0	$0	$250,000	$500,000	$1,000,000
New Product G	Heavily Promote	$0	$0	$0	$0	$500,000
Summary		$0	$200,000	$750,000	$1,250,000	$2,750,000

The development or acquisition of new products and services is one of the ways we can increase our value to our targeted customers, both existing and new. By offering them a greater selection of purchasing options, we stand to capture a larger share of the dollars they spend for the types of goods and services we provide. We may be saving existing client relationships as well, because if our current product offerings are approaching obsolescence, existing customers will begin seeking competitive alternatives. The ability to refresh and enhance our product and service offering is a critical component to meeting our growth projections, and it deserves a regularly scheduled review from us practitioners as part of our planning and budgeting process.

Product Management

We can now begin to visualize what we have to offer, which market segments will be considering our products, and what we are going to propose to fill each of the voids within our current product plan. It is now time to weigh the impact of our overall product management options as they relate to our revenue calculations. We want to be sure to position each of our existing and new product offerings in a manner that makes their benefits easily recognizable to our targeted customers. It is how we position our products (in relationship to our targeted customer's alternative choices) that will become the single most important influence on their buying decision. We need to be very deliberate in how we price, package, and present our product and service offerings.

At a minimum, our target customers should be able to recognize what our products are and what they do. Our customers need to be able to find our products within some familiar business or product category, and our message should be targeted at the users of the product, not necessarily the purchasers of the product. We need to emphasize any differentiating attributes of our product as compared to those of other competitors so that the user can readily see the benefit. And finally, we need to provide reassurance to the ultimate user that if he or she makes a decision to buy our product, we will have the capability and capacity to deliver and support his or her buying decision.

How we brand and promote our offerings will also influence the ultimate user's perception. Branding is important. When many of us think of tissues, we think of Kleenex. The same holds true for many of us when we think of soft drinks, we think Coca-Cola. When the industry thinks of us, we want them to think of the role we play within our industry and the products or services we provide. It is important to validate this identity over and over again within our organizations because changing plans and conditions have a way of diversifying institutions. Our brand is what defines our business and identifies us to others within the industry and marketplace. We are going to be known for something, so our branding and packaging should communicate a common identity and a common theme.

Different product life cycles are going to influence our product management tactics, and our advertising and promotion campaigns need to support these distinctions. In the early stages of new product introduction, we will want to build awareness, so we will undertake an aggressive product promotion campaign. During our products growth stage, we will want to strengthen our distribution capability and stabilize our product pricing. When our products begin to reach maturity, we will want to consider style and design improvements (packaging) and emphasize their proven reliability and market acceptance. And finally, when our products approach their sunset, we will want to reduce our promotion costs and be more willing to make price concessions to extend their market life.

For each one of our major product offerings, we need to develop a competitive positioning matrix (outside of the mother of all matrices). The vertical access of this matrix will represent our relevant sell price, and the horizontal matrix will reflect the features or functionality of the product. We will map our products into this format and compare their position against similar products offered by our identified competitor's to understand how we are perceived in the eyes of the users. This exercise also helps us to recognize our product's strengths and weaknesses, and it gives us a basis for developing our product messaging. Later on in phase 5 of our program we are going to be inputting the output from these comparisons into our mother of all matrices to help us evaluate and decide our tactical choices.

Product Positioning Matrix

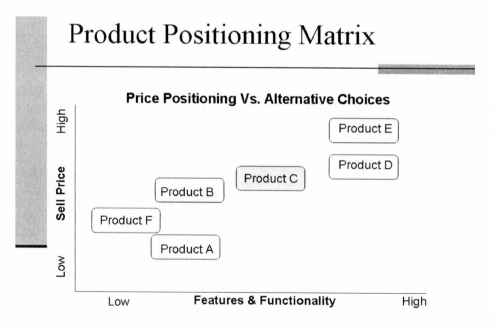

Pricing is another major factor that our targeted customers will consider when making their purchasing decisions. There are two schools of thought for pricing products and services: market-based pricing and cost-based pricing. Market-based pricing attempts to capture the economic value gained from the utilization of a product or service. Cost-based pricing is usually calculated from the costs incurred in producing and distributing a product or service. Both have their place within a pricing strategy, and it is not uncommon for a product plan to contain a little bit of both, depending on the life cycle stages of the products being offered. The newer products will often capture a market value advantage; but as competition enters the race, cost considerations and cost containment begin to play a larger role, and pricing algorithms tend to change.

From the seller's point of view, when our products are sold, we stand to benefit from increased revenues and a decrease or reduction in variable and fixed costs. We also stand to receive intangible benefits, things that we can leverage like industry acceptance or enhanced market reputation. But from the buyer's point of view, our price includes more than just the sticker price. Buyers are considering the cost of ordering or purchasing our product, the actual price or sticker price, any freight or inbound cost, installation costs if required, operating or user costs, future disposal cost, and financing costs if it is large enough to require financing. Our product managers need to be aware of all of this and consider it in arriving at their pricing decisions.

Product & Service Pricing

Sellers Value to Buyer

Buyer's Benefit from Seller +Buyer's Cost From Seller = **Seller's Value to Buyer**
(Additions to Buyer's Gross Profits) (Buyer's Life-Cycle Costs of Seller's Products)

Seller's TOTAL Product	Seller's TOTAL Price

Increase in Revenues	Decrease in Variable costs	Decrease in Fixed Costs	Non Economic Benefits	Ordering Costs	Tag (List) Price	In-Bound Costs	Installation Costs	Operations Costs	Disposal Costs	Finance Costs
1	2	3	4	5	6	7	8	9	10	11

There are other less tangible considerations that go into the pricing equation as well, and they are related to regulatory compliance, component cost variations, and the need to meet changing industry standards. Relative quality is another real consideration, as is warranty and anticipated ongoing support costs. And let's not forget our own organization's threshold for margin contribution if we want to keep our jobs. We cannot possibly address every unique pricing circumstance in this ubiquitous discussion, but here are some checks and balances we can offer to help in communicating price issues.

Try to keep pricing in harmony across like customer groups and manage your volume discount structure consistent with both economic considerations and within legal requirements. Always communicate price changes in a synchronized format to like customers and track the impact of all price changes on market reaction and market share implications. Our products must be readily available for the user to acquire, and they must be priced competitively in relationship to the value received as compared to other available choices. The goal is always to position and present our offerings in a manner where their value is easily recognized by the user.

There are going to be other considerations in the final pricing process that will have an additional effect on product margins, such as cash payment discounts, returns and allowances, warranty obligations, and inventory obsolescence. We have deliberately oversimplified our examples so that the concepts and requirements of product planning, units and dollars, new product introduction, and life cycle management are clearly understood and integrated. If the anticipated number of units to be produced and sold across the various stages of a product's life cycle do not add up to the required revenue expectations, then new products or services have to enter the equation. If new products cannot be added to the mix, then the success of the market plan is likely to be in jeopardy.

There are some generic product management strategies that can be applied to like products, so you may want to consider these guidelines as well. Products with high value unit pricing tend to require a greater sales effort and take longer periods of time to reach their ultimate customer. Because of this, they will have to be offered through very selective channels, and most likely require a variable or negotiable pricing structure. Products with low unit pricing can be more easily standardized, and therefore can be offered through multiple channels with a more stable pricing structure. The former, the higher-priced products, will require a more personalized selling effort, whereas the latter, the lower-unit-priced products, can be distributed through mass selling alternatives.

Channel Selection

It is now time to go channel surfing and begin to select the best methods to reach our identified targeted customers. One of the benefits of building our mother of all matrices is that it helps us to quantify both the total value we expect to receive from each of our product groups and the total value we plan on receiving from selling to each of our targeted customer sets. This provides us with the ability to estimate a dollar figure to work with to pay for our distribution costs. It also helps us to determine the total dollar figure we will have to spend for advertising and promotion. We want to manage these variable expenditures in direct relationship to our expected market segment penetration rates for each of our targeted customer groups.

Our channel choices for the consumer market seem endless, but in fact, they are not. Market research suggests that consumers are reluctant to travel more than five miles from their primary residence to acquire the things they want to buy. That tells us that we either need to have our products available within that geographic circle or available directly to the consumer's primary residence via some other means. We also know that a consumer has a list of shopping experience likes and dislikes that will influence where they are willing to shop. The channels we select must to be able to deal with these customer satisfaction issues, or we could run the risk of not being able to reach our targeted customers.

Things that provide positive influences include

> a variety of shops and goods to experience;
> the structure and layout of certain stores;
> shopping conveniences, restrooms, food courts;
> suitable shopping atmosphere, environment;
> location convenience, access, neighborhood;
> specific brand-name stores;
> specialized services; and
> friendly personnel and people watching.

Things that stimulate negative influences include

> excessive crowd,
> poor architecture or layout,
> restrictive parking,
> limited stores,
> too much walking,

inflexible pricing,
lack of food services,
lack of restrooms, and
impolite personnel.

Consumers will inevitably find a degree of dissatisfaction with some element of the products or services everyone offers as well. Our sales channel contractual arrangements need to address these realities and provide a process for returns and exchanges.

Another consideration in making our channel selection for consumer products is our choice for how we intend to promote or stimulate the market. There are two generic consumer marketing strategies—push and pull. We could select a channel with a strong presence in our targeted geographies (e.g., a well-known department store) through which we can *push* our products by influencing the store's buying and promotion decisions. Or we may choose to select a variety of smaller retail outlets that will provide more of a fulfillment role than a sales role. These smaller outlets would be relying on our advertising and promotion to *pull* our products into the market and influence the ultimate consumer's buying behavior.

Today's consumer is constantly being inundated with product stimulation of one sort or another everywhere they go. Even if the products or services we are providing are something that our targeted customer desperately needs, we will still struggle to get and keep the consumer's attention. So the channel we select is going to have to allow us to provide point of sale promotional materials that enable us to attract the attention of the buyer. We do not want our products on the bottom shelf, but rather at eye level where they can get noticed.

As a result of pulling together our product alignment matrix, we have a fairly good understanding as to which targeted customers are going to buy what set of products and services. We also know, from determining the direct cost elements for those products, how much contribution margin we have available to spend in order to reach the ultimate consumer. The direct-push channels are going to be the more expensive to use as they will want to leverage their purchasing power and market influence. The third-party pull channels, the smaller outlets, will be less expensive to use, but will require us to more aggressively promote our products. We always want our products to be everywhere our targeted customers are, but that is often not practical. We can only match our choices to our pocketbook.

Here are some consumer channel categories to consider:

Chain stores—Nordstrom's, Macy's, Best Buy, Radio Shack
Discount stores—Wal-Mart, Kmart, Costco, Sam's Club
Specialty stores—boutiques, specific product outlets, Golf Smith
Direct order—catalogues and e-commerce

We could also consider letting third parties take our products to these retail groups by electing to work through wholesale distributors. Distributors are traditionally business units that buy and resell merchandise to retailers, other merchants, and commercial users. They do not usually sell to the ultimate consumer. We will have less influence using this channel grouping than we would with the retail group because they are one step further removed from the actual consumer. They will tend to be more reactive to the demands of their customers than proactive in supporting ours, or anyone else's products.

Here are some third-party categories to consider:

Wholesalers—merchants who buy and resell our products
Middlemen or agents—deal makers who tend to follow trends
Brokers—represent both buyers and sellers
Manufacturer's agent—sales agent, paid upon performance
Selling agents—traditionally sell one or more lines of merchandise

Do not underestimate the effectiveness of these third party channels as many industries operate very successfully in this manner. For example, the automotive, furniture, lumber, grocery, and beer and wine industries are all marketed through distribution, and these are all ultimately consumer products.

If we do choose to select wholesalers to distribute our products, they will want to purchase at a reduced prices, so we need to understand the economic implications of their participation in our pricing models. In order for the wholesaler to be a cost-effective channel for us, the cost of using them should be equal to, or less than, the cost of selling and distributing these products directly ourselves. Let's assume that 10 percent of our operating costs are the variable costs we would incur to sell and support our products. If the distributor agrees to perform a portion of these support activities for us, then our internal variable costs should be reduced proportionately. We could then afford to reduce our price to this distributor by a comparable amount, transferring both the responsibility for the product support and the cost to provide this support. So, if our product gross margin is 20 percent, and we avoid a variable cost of 5 percent, then we can afford to sell to this distributor at a 5-percent price discount. If the volumes are comparable, then this could be a good decision for the firm.

We may be considered utilizing other third-party sales channels as well, such as manufacturer's representatives or sale agents. The motivation for this channel is principally to sell as they do not receive any compensation until the sale is consummated. In order to sell, they can often become very aggressive during price negotiations and, if left unchecked, can negatively impact market balance and the margins we need to realize from their effort. In structuring our arrangements with them, we want to be sure to tie their compensation to our margin expectations, and then vary their compensation proportionately. In taking this approach we will vary our cost of distribution through these channels in proportion to the actual gross margin we realize from their efforts. If we adopt a channel of this nature, we need to track and administer this relationship carefully.

Indirect Channel Consideration

Structuring Agents Compensation Arrangement

Customer or End User price				$ 100.00
Expected Gross Margin (20%)				$ 20.00
Agents Commission	@ 100% margin	2.0%		$ 2.00
	@ 90% margin	1.8%		$ 1.80
	@ 80% margin	1.6%		$ 1.60
	@ 75% margin	1.5%		$ 1.50
Contribution to Firm			$15.00 to	$20.00

Always vary compensation to the value of the sale, not the revenue !

For industrial products, the list of channel options becomes a little more complex. In addition to the geographic challenges of reaching our targeted customers, we have the added consideration of the uniqueness of our products. Some industrial products become classified as commodities and can be literally bought and sold out of a catalogue. Others play a more intimate role in the buyer's value chain and need to be specifically engineered, integrated, or customized in order to be desirable. Different types of products are going to require different kinds of channels.

Among the different channel choices to reach industrial clients are

direct sales (the most effective and most expensive);

wholesalers and distributors (the buyers and resellers to others);

original equipment manufacturers, OEM (industrial clients that reuse our product and rebrand it for their customers);

value-added resellers (users who integrate our product into their product or service offerings); and

systems/process integrators (problem solvers who incorporate our wares with others to meet specific applications).

If our products have a high degree of complexity or require that they be integrated into our customer's production process, then we are going to want to represent these products as credibly as we can. This will require us to build, manage, and support a direct-sales effort. The direct-sales channel is the best alternative for these kinds of industrial products because it enables us to obtain direct feedback from the actual users of the product. We can acquire competitive information, information about competitor's products, and feedback about our products that we may need to consider. The challenge for us is to determine how many direct sales associates we will we need and how we should manage their deployment.

There are several options available for us to consider in structuring a direct sales organization, but once again it will depend on the targeted customers we are trying to reach and the complexity of our product offerings. Sales organizations can be structured by geography, by different product groupings, by assigned customer or industry, or any combination of all these. There are advantages and disadvantages to each of these choices, and we will have to determine which alternative is right for us. It will all depend on where our targeted customers are physically located, their requirement for industry knowledge, and the level of support necessary for their success. If we choose to employ a direct sales channel, then we will definitely want our representatives to know what targeted customers to call on and what message to convey.

Industrial Channel Consideration

Direct Sales Force -

Organized by	Advantages	Disadvantages
Geography	Clearly defined Minimizes travel	Breadth of Customers
Product	Product Knowledge & Depth	Breadth of Products
Customer or Industry	Industry & Customer Knowledge	Overlapping territories Travel costs
Common Sales For Multiple Use	Local business ties Minimizes travel	Sales management Different policies
Combination	Maximum Flexibility	Complexity Sales Management

The industrial products that are classified as commodities are best handled through wholesalers and distributors, because the goal for these products is to have them where they are needed, when they are needed, and at a economical price point that is sensitive to market dynamics (supply and demand). This also makes sense from a cost management perspective as well as commodities are generally produced in large quantities to keep down the cost of production. Wholesalers and distributors purchase in bulk (usually barges, railcars, or truckloads), and these arrangements help to keep the wholesale cost system in balance.

For government markets, a business development approach seems to be the most common and most effective channel. To successfully sell to the government, it is often necessary to join larger teams that integrate the capabilities of their company with other organizations to address complex government requirements. One of the critical success factors to participate in this market is the ability to either organize these teams, like the system integrators often do, or effectively contribute on someone else's team. Building these teaming relationships is a much different skill than selling an established product or service, and it usually requires considerably more business or technical savvy. It will also require an investment of time to successfully negotiate these kinds of complex teaming arrangements.

Another approach to selecting a channel for government sales, particularly if we offer an established product, is simply to get on their approved vendors lists and schedules. We mentioned earlier that it is the CCR for the federal government and an approved vendors listing for the state and local governments. Many of these government agencies have purchasing arms (it is the General Services Administration for the federal government) that serve other government agencies, and they can represent our wares via their catalogues. They provide the other government agencies they serve with access to all of the products and services from this providers list. They will catalogue our offerings in their publications and list our products and services to match identified government needs.

As we manage through the channel selection process, we need to constantly remind ourselves that the Internet has changed everything. In the structuring and management of our relationships with our selected channels, we must remain cognizant of the convenience this technology provides to the ultimate customer and how easily today's search engines can find competitive alternatives. It has become a very disruptive factor within the consumer markets, imposing major changes in channel economics. It is also changing the way that industrial clients relate to one another as well, via EDI or e-commerce. As we design our channel relationships, we will need to be clear as to how we will address direct customer contact, how we are going to handle referrals, and how we are going protect the economic models that we are all striving to sustain throughout the distribution chain.

Available Gross Margin

We are going to be returning to our mother of all matrices and add two more categories that will influence our evaluation. For each vertical column, the ones that total up the revenues for each targeted customer segment, we will add a new category at the base entitled total channel cost. We are going to develop a budgeted cost for this category for each of the channels we are considering to reach these market segments. We are striving to get to what is known as the available gross margin, the actual amount of contribution that is earned from each targeted market segment after we have spent all of our marketing effort. This is an extremely important point to make because other than the direct cost to produce the product, all of the other costs associated with getting our products to market are controlled or influenced by us, the marketing professionals.

We will also add a second category that will represent the budget we will allocate to advertising and promotion for each of these customer segments.

For purposes of our hypothetical challenge, we are going to assume that we have been given a total of 10 percent of budgeted revenues by our CFO to manage the entire marketing function. We are going to allocate 5 percent of our forecasted revenues for distribution (channels) and 3 percent of revenues will be set aside for advertising and promotion. The remaining 2 percent will be for other marketing costs. The actual split is immaterial; it is the discipline of the process that is important. Allocating these dollars is not going to be a ubiquitous process as it makes no sense at all to utilize an expensive channel to distribute sunset products to a small segment of the market. A less-expensive alternative should be considered. But the total amount we are going to allocate across all of these categories is fixed; it is all we can afford.

"Mother of All Matrices"

Cost Allocation by Market Segment

Product Groupings	Current Plans	Market A Revenue	Direct Costs	Market A Margin	Other Segments	Plan Yr. # 1
Product Group A	Heavily Promote	$250,000	$175,000	$75,000	xxxxx	xxxxx
Product Group B	Increase Distribution	$1,500,000	$1,200,000	$300,000	xxxxx	xxxxx
Product Group C	Increase Distribution	$1,000,000	$750,000	$250,000	xxxxx	xxxxx
Product Group D	Improve Packaging	$50,000	$30,000	$20,000	xxxxx	xxxxx
Summary		$2,800,000	$2,155,000	$645,000	xxxxx	xxxx
Channel Budget	5% of Revenues			$140,000	xxxxx	xxxxx
Promotion Budget	3% of Revenues			$84,000	xxxxx	xxxxx
Other Marketing Costs	2% of Revenues			$56,000	xxxxx	xxxxx
Available Gross Margin				$365,000	xxxxx	xxxxx

As we return to our mother of all matrices, it is now populated with our existing product lines, our current price points, and an estimate of the number of units and dollars our targeted segments will buy in the current state. We now have to project what this current state might look like over the next five years (our planning horizon) and determine the total revenues that our business-as-usual model could generate for each of the plans and the follow-on years. The difference between our current view (what the model will initially tell us) and our future needs (what the C crowd requires) is the challenge we have to meet. The highlighted areas on the matrix—where we neither have a product identified nor have adequate market coverage—are the obvious targets of opportunity that we can explore to make up the difference.

We are going to start exploring any number of possible scenarios for us to consider and previewing the result across different snapshots in time. We can choose to enter new geographies, new market segments, or new industries with our existing products. If we elect to consider this, then we will need to estimate the added cost of establishing new sales channels and the incremental promotional costs for current and future years. If we elect to accelerate the introduction of a new product line, then we will need to add the additional channel and promotion costs to accomplish this as well. There will be any number of combinations within each time period that could enable us to achieve our plans. We will be making these evaluations and deciding our tactics in the next segment of our program, phase 5.

At one point in my career, I had the opportunity to lead a start-up technology company. This company was founded by two very smart electronic engineers who had an excellent new product concept. They recognized the problem of extending the Internet into rural parts of the country and conceived of a technology to solve this problem. They invented a way to improve existing digital loop carrier system technology to allow for the higher-speed connectivity at the edge of the public switched telecommunications network. This innovative idea was clearly worth investigating, and all that was needed to start the process was some venture capital and the addition of a marketing perspective to explore the business opportunity.

The founders were very capable individuals who understood the technology and how it was to be applied very, very well. But a product is not a product line, and a product line is not a business. Fortunately this new venture brought together a unique blending of skills; as I have a tendency to recognize and value external influences, the founders, the engineers, had a tendency to recognize and value new technical innovation. The combination turned out to be exactly what was needed to get this new company defined and up and running. We still had to do a considerable amount of product requirements planning and business modeling, but eventually we were able to convince the investors to go forward with this new enterprise.

We started by segmenting the market and targeting the smaller independent telephone companies who served these rural communities across the United States. We determined the various technical attributes this new product needed and what these carriers would value. We then determined the technical characteristics and the operational requirements (line sizes) that the product would need to accommodate. We then estimated the numbers of these units that we thought they could purchase, and the price points at which it would be attractive for them to consider. We began to feel better about our future prospects as the process progressed because we were able to quantify a market opportunity and define a set of product requirements that satisfied this identified need. We were able to estimate the value of our company's offerings to these rural operating companies (their purchasing potential) over a defined period of time, and the numbers justified the product development investment.

Even though we did not have to worry about existing products or the life cycles of existing products, we did have to consider all of the other factors highlighted in this segment of the program. We had to map our product ideas to our targeted customers, identify deficiencies that had to be corrected, develop changes and alternatives, introduce them selectively, and then produce and distribute them. To meet our distribution and fulfillment challenge, we selected a prominent outside-plant (wire and cable) distributor as our channel that already had an established relationship with these telephone operators. We supplemented their sales force with our own qualified sales engineers, and the combination proved to be very effective for us.

We essentially built a minimother of all matrices to help us determine our market plan, and we populated it with the same kinds of data that is being hypothetically collected here. We determined what products in what quantities were going to be sold to what customers, and in what time periods. We then scrutinized the different channels we had available to reach these targeted customers and selected the most effective one. We allocated an appropriate amount of dollars to pay for this channel relationship and assigned expectations that enabled us to meet our plans. In other words, we followed the targeted tactics process to connect our business strategy and market plan. We turned strategy into results.

There are no shortcuts, and the effort we are making to discover our targets of opportunity is about to pay dividends. We know where we are currently successful with our existing products, and we have identified other market segments where we could be successful if we choose to go there. We have identified where our product voids are and have defined a process to evaluate and develop new products or replacements. We have also explored our channel options and established some economic parameters to help us select our distribution alternatives. We have pooled our advertising and promotion budget and can reallocate it differently, depending on the tactics we elect to pursue. We have examined and considered a set of generic product management guidelines to help us manage our current—and future-product life cycles. We are now ready to decide the tactics we will employ to accomplish the challenge we have been given.

We will be utilizing the mother of all matrices as our working model to help us evaluate which combination of options gives us the best pathway to success. It is also capable of providing us with any number of contingencies to consider in the event that our preferred course of action should run into unexpected difficulty. When we set our goals and objectives in the next phase of the program, we want to be comfortable that we have more than one path to accomplish them. We will want this flexibility to readjust our priorities and reallocate resources should we have a need to do so. Determining what the final marketing mix is going to be is our job, and we will be introducing a process to help us evaluate our options in phase 5 of our program.

Once again we can relate to our field commander and reflect on where we are in our battle planning. We understand our battlefield (environment and competitive landscape); we are working within our capabilities (development and capacity); and we have selected our targets (targeted customers). We have now enhanced our capability by providing for additional armament (new products) and additional alliances (channels for distribution). We know where we want to go, what we want to deliver, and how we intend to get there. It is now time to organize the effort.

Phase 4 Deliverables

We need to identify the products and services we are considering to offer over the course of our planning horizon. We will specifically address the numbers of units or transactions we are seeking to provide, the targeted price points we will offer them at, and the direct costs associated with providing them.

Sources of information:

> Existing products and service offerings
> Planned product and service offerings
> Considered product and service offerings

We need to construct our market message (positioning strategy) for each of our product groupings, clearly stating the compelling reasons to buy our offer. We will be incorporating this knowledge into our advertising and promotion plans.

Sources of information:

>   Our newly constructed product plan options
>   Competitive product information
>   Market research and industry reviews
>   Trade publications

We need to identify the process and timing of our new product introduction and support plans. Each of our new product introductions has to be managed differently than an established product, and a more deliberate set of actions has to be formalized.

Sources of information:

>   Our newly constructed product plans
>   Our new product-development cycle plans

We need to identify the different channel options to sell, support, and service our offerings. We should be able to clearly articulate why we feel these are our best alternatives, and have an economic model in mind as to how we would contract with them.

Sources of information:

>   Our targeted customer and industry lists
>   Our newly constructed product plans
>   Our identified geographic preferences
>   Our candidate list of potential channels

We can now populate our mother of all matrices with all of the new information we have just learned. We can add units or change sell prices and cost assumptions within our matrix for each year of our plan.

Sources of information:

>   Our newly constructed product plans
>   Our estimates of units and revenues by market segment
>   Our newly selected channel plans and associated costs
>   Our estimates for advertising and promotional costs

The purpose of phase 4 of the program has been to create a framework from which we can determine what our product plan will be and the channel options we will select to distribute these selections. In addition, we have identified and validated where our new product opportunities are and introduced a process to prioritize and develop these new offerings.

Phase 4 Checklist

We have identified a set of product and services that we can provide in sufficient quantity to meet our planned revenue projections.

We have identified the specific number of units, their cost to produce, and the price we could offer them at to various markets during identified accounting periods.

We have constructed a marketing message that positions our products competitively and clearly articulates their value to our targeted customer groups.

We have identified any new products that we want to develop and have established specific product development programs to govern their evolution and introduction.

We have identified the channels we are going to consider to sell and service our offerings, their locations, the targeted customers they will serve, and the economic model by which they will be measured and managed.

We have pooled the budgeted amount of dollars we will have to spend for advertising and promotion of our products and have allocated this amount across our different targeted customer groups within our mother of all matrices.

We have budgeted the channel cost for selling our products and services to each of these targeted groups and have added this cost estimate to our mother of all matrices.

We have populated our mother of all matrices with sufficient information to begin examining different product scenarios to determine the most attractive options for us to consider.

Market Objectives and Resource Plans

Welcome to the world where imagination is the source of value in the economy. It's an insane world, and in an insane world, sane organizations make no sense.

—*Tom Peters*

In phase 5 of our program, we are going to formalize our market plan objectives and decide the tactics that we are going to implement. On our conference table we now have four piles of information, the latest being our product and channel discoveries. On the wall (or loaded into our computer) is our mother of all matrices, and it is populated with products, market segments, and allocated channel and promotional budgets for each group of targeted customers. We have also speculated on what the timing and value of some additional new products might be, and have included these possibilities in our scenario planning. What we need to do next is to adopt a process to help us decide our preferred set of tactics, formally establish our goals and objectives, and then recognize the organizational requirements necessary to achieve them.

Before we can determine our final scenario selections, we must factor in remaining pieces of information that we have to take into account. In phase 1 of the program, we identified our major competitors. Each of these competitors has an established position within the market, and some within the same targeted market segments that we have identified. They are currently providing a comparable product or service and have effective sales channels in place that provide and support their offerings. We are going to have to consider these competitors in the final formulation of our tactical plans so that we spend our resources and energies in the most attractive areas.

We are now going to *decide* the following:

The preferred scenario we will implement with a brief explanation as to why we have chosen this option

Contingency options available to the organization in the event our preferred scenario encounters unforeseen challenges

Our revenue plan, supported by a product plan that quantifies the dollars we will achieve for each year of our plan to reach our stated objectives

Our product plan that specifically addresses the units and dollars necessary to support the revenue plan that we are trying to achieve, including any new products we intend to develop

Our channel plan that specifically addresses the distribution choices we have made to reach each of our targeted customer groups

Our organization plan for the marketing function, assigning specific responsibilities to individuals to support the critical elements of the plan

Our marketing budget, providing a line item accounting of the costs for salaries, expenses, commissions, incentives, advertising, etc.

We have been challenged (in our hypothetical example) to double our market share within the next five years. We discovered, in phase 1 of our process, that our industry is expected to grow at the rate of 10 percent per year. We also discovered that it is presently $100 million in the aggregate, and that it is expected to continue to grow at 10 percent per annum and be $161 million five years from now. In order for us to grow from our existing (hypothetical) 10 percent share ($10 million in revenues) to a 20 percent share in five years ($32 million in revenues), we will need to grow our revenues at an annual rate of 27 percent per year. This growth rate is two and a half or more times faster than the average growth rate of the industry. We will have to generate 17 percent more business than everybody else for the next five years in a row if we are going to meet our stated goal of doubling our market share.

Developing the Market Objective

Revenue Planning:

Our market is expected to grow, in the aggregate, 10% per year
Our industry is expected to follow suit and also grow 10% per year
Total Industry revenues are projected to be $100,000,000 this year
Our Revenues are expected to be $10,000,000 this year, 10% share
We want to increase our market share from 10% to 20% over 5 years

Industry revenues will be $161,100,000 5 years from now
We will need to generate $32,000,000 to attain 20% market share
We have to grow at approximately 27% per year to attain this.

Year 1	Year 2	Year 3	Year 4	Year 5
$12.7M	$16.3M	$20.5M	$26.0M	$32.0M

We are now going to add the competitive information we learned in phase 1 to our mother of all matrices. We will accomplish this by listing each of the major competitors who are active in our targeted market segments at the bottom left of the mother of all matrices (right below our list of products and services). We will then indicate with an X in each of the targeted market segments they are currently active in, and then provide room to total the number of Xs in each column of customers so that we can easily recognize how many competitors are active in each segment. If there are four major competitors active in segment C, but only one is active in segment B, then entering segment B may be more attractive for us. We are going to select our implementation tactics by identifying the path of least resistance. Our goal is to aggressively grow and addressing areas of unfulfilled need is one of our best alternatives.

Secondly, we need to recognize the principal product offerings these competitors provide, and we are going to list them directly below their names. What we want to determine from this exercise is how many product alternatives each targeted group of customers presently has to consider. Just as we would want to target our channels to address unfulfilled market coverage, we would also want to direct our sales efforts to addressing unfulfilled product needs. In phase 4 of our program, we constructed positioning matrices for each of our major products and compared them to our competitor's offerings. We learned from this exercise which of our product offerings competes favorably against our competitors, and which ones struggle. Preferably, we want to focus in those competitive environments where our products have a distinct or perceived advantage.

"Mother of All Matrices"

Market Segments		Consumer Market Targets Potential Value $ "X"			Industrial Market Targets Potential Value $ "Y"		
Competition	Current Plans	Segment A $	Segment B $	Segment C $	Segment D $	Segment E $	Segment F $
Competitor A		X		X	X		
Competitor B			X	X		X	
Competitor C				X	X		
Competitor D				X	X		
# Active		1	1	4	3	1	0

We will now add this last piece of product information to our mother of all matrices by providing additional rows to represent each one of these competitive product alternatives, right below these competitor's names. We will once again place an X in each of the vertical columns (representing our targeted market segments) where these products are being offered. We will allow room to total the number of like product alternatives currently being offered in each one of these market segments. What we are seeking to accomplish from this effort is an understanding of what these targeted customers have available to choose from when they are making their buying decisions. When we identify a market segment where there are a limited number of alternative choices or where our products compete favorably, this is a target of opportunity for us to consider.

We will need a decision tool to help us with this evaluation process so that we take into consideration all of the variables that we have now discovered. We are going to use a tree model for this task because it allows us to continually branch out in many different directions to consider all of the different factors that could affect our success. Our tree suggests that there are three major criteria we must consider and satisfy: opportunity, capability, and profitable execution. Each of these three categories can be subdivided further as we begin to consider additional variables, such as the potential of our targeted customers, our channel selections, and our ability to compete and so forth. Our intent is to make sure that we take into account the appropriate set of considerations as part of our final selection process.

"Mother of All Matrices"

Market Segments	Current Plans	Consumer Market Targets Potential Value $ "X"			Industrial Market Targets Potential Value $ "Y"		
Competition	Current Plans	Segment A $	Segment B $	Segment C $	Segment D $	Segment E $	Segment F $
Competitor A		X		X	X		
Competitor B			X	X		X	
Competitor C				X	X		
Competitor D				X	X		
# Active		1	1	4	3	1	0
Product X		X		X			
Product Y			X	X	X	X	
Product Z				X	X		
# of Alternatives		1	1	3	2	1	0

We are going to look at all of our different scenarios within this decision framework to determine if we have identified the right set of tactics. We are now determining what our market plan is going to be, what our product plan is going to be, what our channel plans are going to be, and what our marketing organization needs to look like to deliver our plans. We are at a point in our program we are finished with data collection and now have to decide what it is we are going to do. Each scenario we are going to consider needs to go through this process so that we select the options with the highest probability for success.

Opportunity

We all recognize that without opportunity there is no chance for success. We are going to validate the opportunities we have identified within our mother of all matrices to determine whether we should pursue them or not. We will start by looking at the blank spaces within our matrix, the areas where there is either a product void, or lack of market coverage. We will use our decision tree to help us determine the different factors we need to consider within these two critical areas. Our first test will be to determine the viability of a selected market segment. Our second test will be to test the attractiveness of the product or service we intend to offer to this targeted group.

Tactical Decision Factors

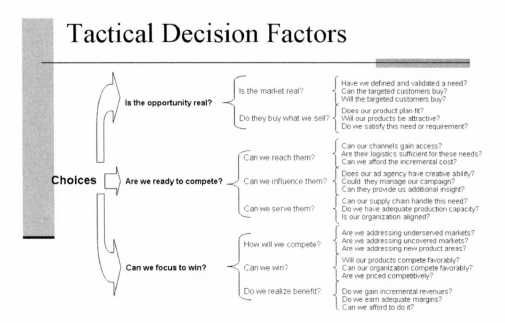

Let's start with a process to validate the targeted market segments we have selected. We know from the work we accomplished in phase 1 of the program that our industry is growing at 10 percent. We identified in phase 3 a set of targeted customers who purchase the kinds of products and services we offer. We further segmented them into different customer groupings to quantify their power buying or purchasing potential. We have subsequently mapped our existing products and services to these targeted customer groups to determine our current state and quantified our business as usual position. When we added up the total of the revenues we could expect from these targeted segments with our current products (the revenue total at the bottom of our vertical columns), we confirmed what our present market position is. (Our current revenues divided by their buying potential provides us with this estimate for our share.)

Everywhere that we do not currently enjoy a market position of at least 10 percent or more would provide a target of opportunity for us to consider. We want to now screen these discoveries to determine whether there really is an opportunity for us to pursue. To accomplish this next step we need to take into consideration other factors that could influence this outcome. So, we test our assumptions further via the next set of branches within our tree model: first, does this group of customers have a *need* or desire to buy what we provide? Second, *can* this customer buy more, or are there financial or logistical restraints? Third, *will* the customer consider buying what we offer? Our tree branches can be further subdivided to consider other factors that may be unique to our individual businesses; but for now, it's understanding the concept that is most important.

The second factor we need to consider in validating our opportunity is whether or not we can satisfy the need identified within this targeted group of customers. Just as we considered the influences that would make their potential attractive to us, they will now be looking at our planned product's ability to meet their business or personal requirements. We have to take a practical look at our ability to market our existing and planned products to these targeted customer groups. We answer this question by following another branch of our tree and examine the next three limbs: First, do the features and attributes of our products satisfy this targeted group's requirements? Second, is our product line packaged and priced in a way that makes it attractive for them to buy?

Third, will it be available in sufficient quantity and within the time frames these customers demand? These initial tree branch considerations will lead to other factors to examine, such as quality, compatibility, reliability, serviceability, pricing, and financing schemes, etc. It's understanding the concept that is important for now.

In phase 2 of our program, we catalogued each of our current product offerings and determined where they were in their respective life cycles. In phase 3 of our program, we identified the targeted customer groups that we want to sell to, whom in the aggregate, possess more than enough purchasing power to enable us to achieve our new revenue objectives. In phase 4, we populated our mother of all matrices with the current state product offerings and assigned units and dollars to each of the targeted customer groups. And, in phase 5, we just identified market segments where our customers have a lesser number of competitive products to choose from. Everywhere that there is a minimal number of competitive products or a market segment that does not currently purchase what we offer provides us with the potential to introduce additional products and services.

We are not going to know our success rate on these fronts until we get out into the market place and experience the unique requirements of the customers we are trying to serve. But we can make some intelligent guesses and return to our mother of all matrices to quantify their impact. For every void we are seeking to address, we can enter our guesstimate for the number of units and dollar value these new product sales could provide. These assumptions will be populated in the same fashion as our original product line was, and when we add up the differences, we will discover what the impact each of these alternatives is worth. Needless to say, the timing of these events is going to be different by market segment and by product availability (new product development cycles), so we have to make intelligent allowances for these variables.

We also need to recognize the impact of these choices on other parts of our marketing mix. The introduction of a new product normally requires a heavy advertising and promotion campaign to launch it. We have to recognize this fact and, once again, find a way to allocate a sufficient amount of budgeted dollars to this effort without exceeding the total we have to work with. We accomplish this by reducing the allocations we have provided for mature products or saturated market segments and move these dollars to our new products and newly targeted segments. Every opportunity we identify from our mother of all matrices needs to be considered in this fashion.

Once we determine that a selection of our targeted customers have a need for what we intend to offer, have the ability to buy it, and can be influenced to consider it, we then have to determine if this approach is worth considering. We return to our mother of all matrices and allocate more of our existing or planned product units into this identified scenario to determine what the incremental value of this choice could be. We need to fairly estimate the cost to penetrate this new area of the market and make allowances for this new requirement. If we are going to choose this alternative we have to accommodate this incremental expense from somewhere else within our marketing mix. Our final choices will be influenced by the amount of incremental available gross margin we can generate from each new scenario as compared to the cost we would incur to execute it.

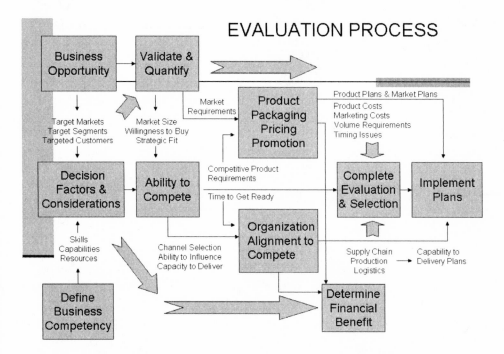

EVALUATION PROCESS

CAPABILITY—

In phase 2 of our program, we conducted an internal analysis of our organization to determine if there were any limitations preventing us from growing at an accelerated rate. We informed other members of the management team to start considering the adjustments they would need to make within their own functional areas. In addition, we examined our own marketing organization to determine whether or not we had sufficient capability to support the marketing challenge we have just been given. We are getting ever closer to knowing what products we are going to provide for what markets and in what quantities and what time frame. Now, we have to organize the effort and select the structure necessary to accomplish the task.

We all recognize that without the right organization and support structure in place our efforts will inevitably fall short. We will once again utilize our decision tree to help us determine the critical pieces we need to put in place. We are going to be critically dependent on three factors: First, the sales channels we will select to reach our targeted customers. Second, our ability to promote awareness and create demand for our product offerings. Third, our capacity to produce and deliver the sufficient quantities of products needed within the required time frames. Even if we have determined that an existing product set would be attractive to a new market segment, we can't consider this option if we cannot find a reliable sales channel or produce the incremental amount of product needed to serve it. We have to know these answers in advance.

We start by selecting the right channels to present our products to the right customers. In phase 4 of our program, we identified the different kinds of channels that we would consider to reach different groups of customers. We now have a better understanding of both the quantity of product and the different kinds of products we are going to offer to each of our targeted market segments. This now allows us to screen our potential channel candidates further to insure that they can meet our three critical criteria: First, they either have or can gain access to our targeted customers. Second, they have the capacity to support our volume requirements and logistical needs. Third, they can accommodate our revenue requirements within our established cost guidelines.

The less complex a product or service is, the easier it is going to be to market it through indirect channels; the more complex the product, the greater the need for additional or direct support. If our product line has relatively few unique characteristics, then the amount of investment required to position and promote it should be kept to a minimum. We should be looking for the least expensive channel to get it to the largest number of users, most likely a wholesaler or distributor. If we are offering a highly technical product that is integrated into the production of our targeted customer's products and services, then we are going to require a direct sales effort that can explain its unique characteristics and a fulfillment organization to support it.

Once again, we will use our decision tree to help us make the right selections for the right reasons. Each of our initial tree branches will divide further to reveal other areas of the relationship that we will want to consider. Things such as contract terms, service level agreements, inventory stocking commitments, repair, and exchange support, etc. Once we have decided on the who, we are going to select for each market segment; then we need to decide on the how many. The *how many* question is answered simply with math.

We know how much volume we need for each year of our plan, we know which products will provide it, and we know which targeted customer groups we have targeted. So if channel A can only handle certain geographies or certain products, then we go looking for other channels to fill the void. It is conceivable that we could wind up having different channels for different products serving different industry segments in different geographies. Whatever our final channel selection turns out to be, we have to manage it so these choices will also affect our staffing plans.

Developing the Channel Plan

Channel Assignments to Support Revenue Growth:

	Yr 1	Yr 2	Yr 3	Yr 4	Yr 5
No. of Distributors	1	2	2	3	3
Expected per Channel	$5.0	$5.0M	$5.0M	$5.0M	$5.0M
No. of Direct Sales	4	5	6	7	8
Expected Per Rep	$2.0M	$2.2M	$2.5M	$2.5M	$2.5M

| Total Assigned | $13.0M | $20.8M | $25.0M | $32.5M | $35.0M |

We will need to promote the awareness of the products we are bringing to market, so we have to be diligent in the selection of our advertising choices to enable this. We are always interested in the awareness that advertising promotes, but what we are really focused on is influencing the ultimate buying decision. In selecting an advertising firm, we want to be sure to consider the following:

The quality of their creative strategies
Their ability to manage proposed campaign plans
Their ability to provide any additional market knowledge
Their media connections and ability to plan and place our ads

We are looking for any additional value adds they can offer us to enhance our market plan success.

Our media plans need to have a clear and specific objective, which will be derived from our market planning, not theirs. We will instruct the advertising agency as to who the targeted customers are, who we are trying to reach, and where they need to contact them. We also need to agree on what the media strategy is going to be to reach these targeted customers. Are we going to use TV, radio, magazines, newspapers, or something different? We want to be sure and obtain agreement on the *how*, not just the *what*. And finally, we want a clear understanding on the implementation tactics—the content and the timing of our advertising campaign. It is our campaign, not the ad agency's; and we should insist on controlling its execution.

We will utilize our decision tree to help us sort through the different advertising and promotion options that are available to us. We will be relying heavily on their capability to get our message into the right markets at the right time. We want assurances that this can be accomplished within our required time frames and for the allocated budget amount we are willing to spend. We may have additional needs for trade show collaterals, media support, internal promotion campaign support, product posters, and the like. The timely promotion of our products and market plans is another critical success factor for us. This needs to be well thought through.

Once we are satisfied that we can represent (channels) and promote (advertising and promotion) our products, we need to make sure that we can actually deliver them to where they are needed. It is time to take a deeper look into the different segments of our product delivery system to insure that the critical components are in place. Our decision tree suggests that we are going to be dependant on the successful alignment of first, our supply chain for component parts; second, our production capacity to produce sufficient quantities; and third, logistics, to deliver the product to where it is needed when it is needed. There will be other elements of the order entry and delivery process to align (such as customer care and information processing systems), but for right now we are concentrating on our physical product delivery needs.

Depending on the size of the organization we are part of, these diverse functions could be managed by other work groups within our firms. We are about to become the coordination point, the orchestra leader so to speak, and we are going to be managing the information flow between supply and demand. As we finalize our market and product plans, we will be providing a product forecast to these stakeholder groups that represent our anticipated needs for an identified period in time. We will be required to provide a "rolling forecast" of our product needs monthly, that covers a defined period (usually ninety days forward) so that others can meet our requirements. Our forecast is going to identify the number of units we need, by product, and arrange for them to be stored or delivered to a place that can accommodate our customer's demands.

These other parts of the organization will in turn be making adjustments to their facilities and staffs based on the information we supply them. We are going to be placing ever-increasing demands on this group to increase production, expand and streamline logistics, and improve turnaround and delivery cycles. Production may have to arrange for new suppliers and possibly additional shifts. Warehousing may need to open new facilities, and shipping may have to establish new delivery capabilities. Needless to say, our market and product plans are going to have a tremendous impact on what the rest of the organization does, how they organize, and how much they spend. No pressure here!

Our intentions for capacity planning are to make sure that we have developed a procedure to insure this alignment. We have to formally chart the information flows between our marketing function and our internal support structure and determine who is responsible to provide what information, in what format, and in what time frame. Equally important is to understand who is responsible to react to the information once it is received and what is it that we all expect them to do with it. These requirements are going to vary from company to company, product set to product set, but unless we can do it all ourselves (and nobody can), we have to work through this. The more definitive and automated we can make this process, the better we are going to be able to respond to our customer's increasing demands.

We spoke earlier in phase 2 of the program about how communication leads to collaboration, and that collaboration leads to success. Process definition has a way of improving communication between different functions, particularly within large organizations. Taking the time to define how the organization is going to respond to this increasing demand (27 percent or more additional volume per year) for incremental products and services will mitigate future customer disappointments. Flowcharting how our supply chain, production, and logistics are going to accommodate these new demands is another critical success factor.

Execution

We have now identified where the opportunity is for us within our market segments, and we are comfortable that our products would be welcomed there. We have selected our advertising firm to promote our efforts and selected our sales and distribution channels. We are comfortable that we have put a system in place to communicate our capacity needs and that the supporting parts of the organization will be responsive to our ever-changing requirements. It is now time to specifically choose the tactics we are going to employ to achieve the results we desire. We have three more things to consider before we finalize our plans. First, our competitor's activities in each of these targeted areas. Second, whether or not we can win in these selected environments. Third, will we realize the economic benefit we want as a result of the effort?

When we added competitive information to our mother of all matrices, we recognized the number of active competitors in each of our targeted market segments. We subsequently recognized their comparable product offerings and mapped these product groups to our targeted market segments as well. As we examine each of the tactical choices we are considering, we want to make sure that we select those environments where we have the best opportunity to compete. So we will return to our decision tree and explore the next set of branches that ask, are we entering an underserved market? Are we going to be entering a previously uncovered market? Are we going to be addressing a market area where we believe our products have advantage? We must be able to validate our choice to address this segment.

If we believe the environment is right for us, then we need to ask the next set of questions to help us zero in on what it is we are going to do. Our next set of tree branches asks: Can our products compete favorably? Can our company compete favorably? Can we meet the price expectations of this selected group? In other words, we are about to spend incremental resources to go sell to this group of targeted accounts, and we want to assess in advance our chances of winning their business. If our product plan fits their needs, if our pricing can be competitive, and if we have the organizational capability to meet their operational demands, then we want to go there.

And that brings us to the final and last consideration in our selection process—financial considerations. Every possible scenario we will consider will have an impact on the existing organization's structure and resulting operating costs. For example, making a choice to enter N—new geographies with a line of consumer products—could be as simple as selecting a regional department store, striking an acceptable distribution or resale model, and creating an introductory advertising and promotion campaign. However, if we are considering opening our own retail outlets, then we are looking at a need for much more advanced planning. This could require the spending of advanced advertising and promotion costs, and making provisions for deploying inventory and staffing to each of these new outlets.

We will once again return to our mother of all matrices and populate each of these variables for each of the scenarios we are considering to determine their value and effect on our overall plans. We want to be sure that we can address three more branches of our decision tree: Do we gain the required incremental revenues we need? Do we earn adequate margins from these incremental sales? Can we afford the incremental cost to acquire these new customers? Our matrix is deliberately designed to allow us to vary our price assumptions, our penetration rates by market segment, our advertising and promotion expenditures, and our sales channel costs. As we consider each of the identified targets of opportunity we have discovered, we populate our matrix with these variables and evaluate what the benefits and trade-offs are to pursue it.

One of the other benefits of this process will be the discovery of areas or activities where we have redundancy and duplicate efforts. As we move forward in the final selection process we are going to be reallocating our operating budgets to support the new directions we want to take. Discovering that duplicate dollars were spent in one area that can now become available to support a new growth area helps to strengthen our efforts. We could also discover areas of channel conflict, market segments where we have one or more channel competing for the same business. This is not always a bad thing, but it should be a conscious decision if we allow it. We only have so many dollars to spend, so putting them where they can produce the highest returns is the name of our game, and paying multiple channels may not be prudent.

Goals and Objectives

We have enough information assembled and sorted on our conference table, and displayed in our mother of all matrices to begin quantifying our market plans and corresponding operating budgets. Our plan must clearly support the stated goals and objectives of the total organization, and specifically state what it is we are going to accomplish. We are going to double our market share within five years by growing our business at the rate of 27 percent or more per annum. As a result of this effort, we will become the market share leader within our industry and be recognized as the number one provider of the kinds of products and services we provide. Our direction and objectives must now be translated into quantifiable goals for revenues, contribution, and customer satisfaction.

We do this by recapping units and dollars as we did earlier, only this time, we are going to reflect the changes in these quantities that are necessary to achieve the revenues we want. Our market objective, for year one of our plan, is to grow 27 percent or more from our present revenues of $10 million, so our new requirement is going to be $12.7 million. Our supporting product plans, units to be sold, have got to be aligned to produce this $12.7 million objective. We validate this within our mother of all matrices by adding up our vertical columns for each market segment and then totaling their combined effect. We further validate this by adding up each of our horizontal product rows to determine the value of each set of products we will offer, and then total their combined value. These two totals should be the same, and it confirms that we have now identified the appropriate amount of products to be sold to an identified group of customers in support the revenues we plan to achieve in year one.

We are going to continue to repeat this process over and over again to develop the different scenarios for years two, three, four, and five of our plan. We want to establish as many rational routes to accomplishing these goals as we can, and having more than one option is important. As each scenario is considered, we will populate our matrix with the associated variables and push the "total buttons" over and over again. If the result allows us to achieve our stated goals, then it is one of the options we should consider. If the total comes up short, then it is not a viable consideration, and we should discard it. It is much less expensive to play the what-if game within this controlled environment than it is to discover the pitfalls of poor choices later on in the operating environment.

This is a critical point in our market planning because it is here that our dependency on new product revenues or new customer acquisition will become apparent. Our existing products may not be adequate to attain our market share goal, so we will become dependent on the proposed new product offerings to garner new revenues and approach new customers. The coordination of this revenue timing sequence with the projections for each new product development cycle is essential. If the new products cannot get to the market within these budgeted time frames, then the expected revenues are not going to be achieved; and contingencies will have to be identified as part of this process.

Our final version of this effort is going to be the product and revenue plan we will submit to the C crowd for approval. For each year of our plan, we have now identified the products we intend to sell, the actual number of units we will supply, and the prices we intend to offer them for. When we add it all up, it provides us with the total revenues we need to accomplish our growth objectives for each year of our plan. This will become our official product and revenue plan, and we will be communicating this with other parts of the organization so that they can, in turn, make adjustments to their functional areas to support these new volumes. It will also become the blueprint from which we will address all other elements of our marketing mix.

Developing the Revenue Plan

Product Plans to Support Revenues:

		Yr 1	Yr 2	Yr 3	Yr 4	Yr 5
Product A	Units	10000	15000	20000	25000	30000
(New Product)	Price	$250	$240	$235	$230	$225
	Revenues	$2.5M	$3.6M	$4.7M	$5.75M	$6.75M
Product B	Units	20000	25000	30000	35000	40000
	Price	$300	$305	$310	$315	$320
	Revenues	$6.0M	$7.6M	$9.3M	$11.0M	$12.8M
Product C	Units	10000	12000	15000	21000	27500
	Price	$420	$425	$433	$440	$453
	Revenues	$4.2M	$5.1M	$6.5M	$9.25M	$12.45
TOTAL Revenues		$12.7M	$16.3M	$20.5M	$26.0M	$32.0M

In the next segment of the program, we will be introducing governance systems and identifying the activities that will drive our desired results. The management of our sales channels is one area that will come to the forefront because we are dependent on their success for our success. As we begin to calculate the cost structure to execute our plans, we need to recognize that the channels will be developing incremental new business in advance of us actually fulfilling orders and recognizing revenues. This would suggest that the cost or a portion of this cost will be incurred in advance of the revenues that they generate. Our proposed budgets will need to reflect this timing issue.

As we decide our final scenarios, we want to make sure that we have considered all of the other cost elements that our organization is going to incur in accomplishing this new revenue objective. Other parts of the organization need to review supply chain implications, production issues, processing capabilities, and logistics. We can now share with them that we will have to produce *n* number of different product units, within a given time frame. We will have to service a new product offering that looks like this, process *n* number of orders, and so forth. They should all now have quantifiable data to work with to address their own specific needs. Some of these incremental costs will be direct costs and go into the product cost category of our product plan, and others will be infrastructure costs that will need to be added to the overhead and operating budgets of these functional groups.

Our planning work has one more step to complete as we now have to determine what our marketing organization will look like and how we will spend our budgeted dollars. Determining how much we can afford to spend for each or our budgeted categories is the first step. Once we know the total dollars we have available, we can then allocate them across each of our different marketing categories as the second step. We will get some help from the CFO's office (chief financial oficer) as he or she will be issuing guidelines outlining what our organization has allotted for us. All we want to know is what our allocation is; we will determine the best way to spend it.

For purposes of our hypothetical example, we have assumed that the CFO is allocating no more than 10 percent of budgeted revenues to pay for the entire marketing effort. We have elected to spend 50 percent of these funds (5 percent of revenues) on sales, distribution, and fulfillment; 30 percent (3 percent of revenues) on advertising and promotion; and the remaining 20 percent (2 percent of revenues) on staff and staff functions. The actual breakdown is not important; it is the deliberate decision making that comes from it that is. Whatever we are going to allocate to internal costs will be a relatively fixed expense throughout our planning horizon. The costs we choose to allocate to distribution and promotion are going to be variable. This is a very, very important point because we are going to set an expectation in the next segment of the program, phase 6, that these costs be managed in proportion to the revenues generated within the market segments they are allocated to.

In considering our own organizational needs, we should identify and assign the marketing functions we plan to perform. The activities within the marketing organization that are generally required are as follows:

Function	Where Performed
set policies, goals, and objectives	marketing management
identify markets, products, services	market research/management
determine competitive standing	market research/management
forecast revenues	marketing and sales channels
recommend product and packaging specs.	product and market managers
select distribution channels	marketing management, research
develop strategy and tactics	marketing manager w/GM
short-range goals and objectives	marketing management
prepare operating budgets	marketing management w/GM
recommend and set pricing	marketing and product managers
training and development	product managers and others
order processing et al	marketing, operations, logistics
credit and collection practices	sales, marketing, finance
customer service and support	customer care, tech support
execution and administration	marketing management et al
long range planning and adjustments	marketing management with GM

Our marketing organization will be designed to compliment the business we are in and the organization that we are part of. For example, an industrial business that focuses on vertical markets with a direct sales channel will look different than a consumer business that may have multiple distribution channels to reach disparate geographies. Organizations that can offer similar products to similar customer groups have a greater opportunity to share resources and leverage advertising and promotion expenditures. Larger organizations that serve multiple business units will look still different, as they may need to focus their resources more specifically for different product groupings and different customers.

Let's recap to make sure that we have identified everything we need:

We have calculated our revenue goals and confirmed that they are consistent with the planner's expectations for market share growth (from 10 to 20 percent over five years).

We now know how rapidly we have to grow year over year to reach this market share objective within the five-year planning horizon (27 percent per annum) and have developed our revenue plan to support this.

We know which targeted customers we are going to pursue, their potential value, and the affordable channels we are going to use to reach them (5 percent of our anticipated revenues has been allocated for this).

We have identified and mapped the products we are going to provide to each targeted grouping and quantified the number of units of each product or service we plan to sell, its direct cost and gross margin.

We have determined our advertising and promotion plan to provide life cycle support for our existing and planned product line and market expansion efforts (3 percent of revenues has been allocated for this).

We have used the remainder of our dollars (2 percent of budgeted revenues) to organize and staff our marketing department to provide the different functions that we have identified as necessary for us to deliver our plan.

As we select our final choices, we must consider the unknowns that could inevitably affect the outcome of our plans. It is for this reason that we will present a *best-cast*, *worst-case*, and *most-likely* market plan to the C crowd. We want to introduce the possibility that if our new product development efforts are late, or if our market penetration estimates do not materialize, then we could potentially come up short. We will be signing up to and measuring ourselves against the most-likely scenario, but we will also acknowledge that with a little luck, some unanticipated good things could also happen. As part of this discussion, we will be prepared to discuss one or more of the contingency options we discovered as part of our scenario planning (the what-ifs we calculated within the mother of all matrices.)

We can now create our "official" commitments for our revenue plan, product plan, and contribution targets. We will assign and/or contract with our direct sales channels and distributors to sell the revenues per year that we require to achieve our goals. We will design our marketing staff organization adding to it the skills or positions necessary to manage our planned activities. We will develop our operating budget and contract with our external advertising or research firms for the support we require. Now we just need to add it all up, compare it to business as usual and reassure ourselves that if we follow the plans and programs we have just developed, we will achieve the goals and objectives we have set for ourselves.

As field commanders, we now have our battle plan. We know our environment (economic and industrial climate, competitive landscape) and where we want to go (targeted market segments and customers); we know how we are going to get there (channel plans); we know what we are taking with us (product plans); we know what skills we need to make the journey (resource plans); and we know what we want to achieve (market share and revenue growth). What we have left to build is our command-and-control center (measurement systems) that will enable us to assess our progress on each front and govern the prudent use of our precious resources.

Phase 5 Deliverables

We need to run our different scenarios through the mother of all matrices and determine which set of products and targeted customers give us our best opportunity for success. We will formalize three different perspectives, our best case, our worst case, and our most-likely case. It is the later, the most-likely case that we will establish as our formal market plan.

Sources of information:

> Our mother of all matrices from which will come our plans
> Our product plans, which have provided us with current and future products
> Our planning assumptions from phase 1 and phase 2, which have quantified our opportunities, identified our competitors, and determined our capabilities
> Our decision tree and evaluation process

We next have to declare the channels we are going to utilize to distribute and support our offerings. This should be directly aligned with the targeted customer segments we have selected to pursue and the geographies that we have identified as desirable.

Sources of information:

> Our product and channel options from phase 4
> The revenue and product plans we just developed in phase 5
> The channel economics we have determined
> Our decision tree and evaluation process

We next need to identify our advertising or promotional budget to support the effort we have just formalized. New products going to new markets will be more costly to promote; established products with established customers will be less costly to support.

Sources of information:

> Allocation of expense dollars assigned to company's operating budget
> Product and channel plans from phase 4 and phase 5
> Revenue plans by market segment
> Our decision tree and evaluation matrix

We next need to organize and budget our marketing organization and identify the positions we will fill to support our marketing mix.

Sources of information:

> Product and channel plans from phase 4
> Revenue and growth plans we just established
> Allocation of expense dollars from company's operating budget
> Organization design and structure determined by tactics adopted
> Organization of our marketing mix costs so that they can be allocated
> proportionately to each of the market segment operating statements
> we have created

The purpose of phase 5 of our program has been to decide the actual combination of activities and events that we are going to pursue in order to achieve our stated goals and objectives. We have selected our targets of opportunity and screened these tactical choices through a decision process that validated the opportunities they provide, recognized our requirements to participate, and quantified their value to our firm.

Checklist

> Description of scenarios identified to pursue
> Description of contingencies, best case, worst case
> Formalized revenue plan reflecting growth objectives
> Formalized product plan to support the revenue projections
> Formalize channel plans reflecting expectations and costs
> Formalized promotional plans reflecting allocations and cost
> Populated operating budgets consistent with CFO's requirements

PHASE 6

Monitor and Measure Results

The way you activate the seeds of your creation is by making choices about the results you want to create. When you make a choice, you mobilize vast human energies and resources which otherwise go untapped. All too often people fail to focus their choices on results, and therefore their choices are ineffective. If you limit your choices only to what seems possible or reasonable, you disconnect yourself from what you truly want, and all that is left is compromise.

—Robert Fritz

In phase 6 of the program, we are going to establish the levers and gauges that will help us to achieve our marketing plan. We have deliberately chosen the word *govern* over the word *manage* because we tend to interpret management as more of a controlling function than a contributing function. But when we are governing, we are not only in touch with the results, but we are also engaged in the activities required to achieve those results. As the owners of the market plan, we have to be able to influence these activities. We will want to know what things are going well, what things need to be adjusted, and what things may need to be changed altogether.

Our governance model should provide visibility into the following areas:

The traditional administrative profit and loss statements reflecting revenues, adjustments and returns, cost of goods sold and gross margins

A comparison to prior years, along with year to date calculations to enable the calculation of revenue growth rates

The traditional departmental operating budget reflecting salaries and expenses, line item recognition for advertising and other expenses

A collection of product plans reflecting numbers of units and revenues generated by individual products rolled up into product summaries

A series (or just one) of product development plans and stage gates outlining the timing and expectation of these new introductions

A collection of channel reports, reflecting the assignment of product units and revenue dollars to each channel and their current performance

A sales channel feedback system that enables the collection and dissemination of customer feedback to product and market managers

A virtual P&L statement by market segment reflecting revenues, cost of goods sold, gross margin, and contribution with a comparison to budget for each of these targeted segments

We will begin building our measurement systems by identifying the two major categories of reports we will want to generate. First, are the traditional administrative and financial measurements that track all of the financial indicators: revenue, cost of goods, gross margin, contribution margin, salaries, expenses, and others. Our CFO will provide this information in a format that compares our reported results to the operating budgets we established in phase 5 of the program. Secondly, we will want to create an additional set of operating measurements that will provide visibility into the performance of our products, promotion programs, and channel selections. We will also want to measure contracted sales against established channel expectations (quotas) and our customer reactions to the campaigns we will be introducing.

The administrative tracking systems will be compliant with whatever formats our CFO has adopted to track those items within his or her established chart of accounts. We should be confident that this recognition of revenues and costs will be "consistently applied and compliant with the Federal Accounting Standards Board and Generally Accepted Accounting Principles." Every month this group will produce an actual budget variance report and everyone with a management title will get to see how well we are tracking to these recorded items. For the most part, this information is an excellent tool to help us manage our expenses, and see how well we did during a prior period against our budgeted plans. But these reports cannot impact the future, they can only report the financial impact of what has already occurred in the past.

What we want to establish is how well we are progressing toward achieving the market plan we just submitted to the C crowd in advance of the C crowd receiving the reported results. The scenarios we selected from our mother of all matrices have enabled us to choose our preferred course and direction. So let's take a look at what we said we were going to accomplish (hypothetically) in order for us to grow our business and double our market share.

> We need to gain access to new groups of targeted customers.
> We need to increase our volumes with our existing customers.
> We need to establish additional sales channels to sell the new volumes.
> We need to introduce promotion campaigns to support these sales.
> We need to manage these activities within our economic guidelines.
> We need to sell n units of product groups A, B, C, and D.
> We need to introduce n number of new products and services.
> We need to generate n amount of revenues and n amount of margin from these product sales within budgeted time frames.
> We need to establish effective logistics for fulfillment and support.
> We need to grow revenues at 27 percent or more per annum to gain market share.
> We need to increase our market share from 10 to 20 percent.
> We need to improve our industry ranking from number n to m.

By accomplishing all of the above, we should be a success! Piece of cake!

The approach we recommend to governing this many activities at once is to examine each of the goals and objectives we have set for ourselves and determine what the critical path is to accomplish them. In phase 5 of the program, we introduced a decision tree to help us identify all of the variables we needed to consider as we made our final tactical choices. What we are going to do now is establish a similar *tree model* to help us identify the sequence of events we will need to follow to attain these goals and objectives. Even though there are numerical indicators that are equally important to establish, building these initial milestone expectations is the best way to get things started on the right track.

We are going to develop our critical paths with the help of this tree structure and approach it in a similar way that program managers build their project plans. We will begin by identifying the end result we want to accomplish, establish the time frames in which we want to accomplish them, and then work backward to identify all of the things we must do to enable these events to happen. So our tree starts with the accomplishment; it branches into a set of milestones that support this accomplishment, then further divides into a set of activities that need to occur, and further branches out to form the individual tasks that must be assigned and performed.

Critical Path for Tactical Achievement

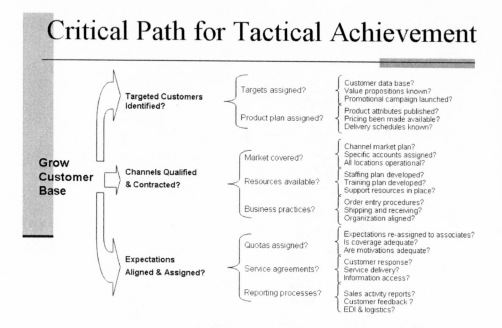

Let's start with our first objective—expanding our customer base. We should already know the names, addresses, and purchasing habits of our existing customers; but just in case we don't, here is a checklist. At a minimum we should know the company's name, their address, the channels we have assigned to them, our purchasing contact, and how to reach them (phone, e-mail, fax). We also should know what they buy from us, how frequently they purchase, and the value of those purchases to our firm. Ideally, we would want to deposit all this information into a database that we can sort by dollar volume, products, locale, industry codes, etc. Remember, our planning assumption is that we can increase our volumes with these existing customers as well, so we need to track our progress on a customer by customer basis.

If we are selling consumer products through established retail outlets, then we will need to build a different kind of data collection system. We would want to establish a method to capture customer data at the point of sale where the purchase actually takes place. Many of the larger retailers have sophisticated check out technology that enables the capture of customer demographics at this checkpoint, and their systems can correlate this information with our products and service offerings. We need to utilize this information to help us measure and track our retail sales volumes through these outlets to our targeted customers. We will also want to closely watch how our inventory flows through these larger retail outlets, as bulk purchasing can often disguise where our products are actually going, and this could impair our visibility to the ultimate consumer's buying patterns.

We want to track our progress toward capturing newly identified targeted customers as well; the ones we are counting on to incrementally grow the business. We will want to know whether or not our channels are able to reach them and whether or not our channels were successful in obtaining initial orders. This is going to require us to develop a progress reporting capability so that we can be aware of the efforts of these channels, and not just the results of their efforts. The point of collecting and recording this information is to validate our planning assumptions as we implement. We either can reach these targets or we can't, either they can buy or they can't, either they will buy or they won't. As we execute down this critical path and discover that a selected group of customers is not going to be viable for us, we will have to return to our mother of all matrices and select an alternative group.

We are going to follow our tree model backward from our stated goal of expanding the customer base to identify the first set of milestones we need to accomplish: (1) targeted customers identified, (2) channels assigned and contracted, and (3) expectations assigned. Each of these activities will require us to take additional steps to insure that they are executed in support of our plans. For example, just assigning expectations doesn't necessarily mean that they will be met. We will want to insure that these sales channels have added sufficient staff, completed adequate product training, and have adopted our required reporting processes. We are going to be tracking the completion of the required tasks that need to be completed in addition to the quantitative measurements that result from these actions. If the critical tasks necessary to support the goal do not happen, the results will never materialize.

So, our measurement system for increasing the number of customers we have to sell to has to be able to track not only our sales results, but our sales efforts. If we have a direct sales organization, we will need a sales call reporting system, such as Sales Force Management (www.salesforce.com), or something similar to track our activities. If we are selling through distribution, we would want a similar activity report, except that the information fields will look a little different. If we are selling through established retail outlets, then we will require them to collect and report point of sale information (product, price, store location, and the name and zip code of the actual purchaser.) We want to know as early in the process as we possibly can whether or not we are reaching our targeted customers instead of discovering later on that sales to them never materialized.

Our second objective is to grow our revenues with existing customers, and this requires us to pay attention to the traditional sales management matrices. We will pay attention to the number and value of proposals submitted, sales consummated against expectations, and backlog reports (booked orders that have yet to ship). We will pay particular attention to the volume of new product proposals we generate, their value, and the actual number of orders received. We invested in these new product concepts in anticipation of attaining additional volumes from our existing customer base and want to measure our progress in this regard. Watching the trends of these numerical factors enables us to predict future revenues and gives us a feel for how accurate our planning assumptions were.

If we are relying on a direct sales force to deliver our message and support our new products, then we need a system to measure their effectiveness. Measuring a direct sales effort is not as simple as assigning quotas and hoping for the best. The actual cost of hiring, training, supervising, and supporting a new sales representative is usually about twice the amount we are going to pay them during their first year. How well we organize and align our direct sales effort (as well as the type of compensation and motivation programs we chose) will all have a significant impact on their performance. In phase 3 of the program, we spent a considerable amount of effort selecting our potential customers, so we need to make sure that our direct sales effort is structured to cover all of these identified targets and trained to represent our new product offerings.

There are five questions we should ask ourselves when we attempt to measure our sales force's effectiveness. First, is the sales force structured correctly to physically reach our targeted customers? Second, is the sales force staffed with the right kinds of people to represent our products (sales vs. sales engineers)? Third, are we providing the appropriate guidance and focus for the group? Fourth, is there adequate sales and product support available for them? Fifth, does our sales compensation program drive the desired behavior we want? If all we do is assign quotas and then simply criticize those who do not meet these objectives, we will accomplish nothing but turnover and be forced to start the process all over again. Our measurement system has to take into consideration our tactical choices, and then constantly adjust to the new marketplace realities that we are inevitably going to discover.

Measuring Channel Effectiveness

Five Questions to Ask in Assessing Sales Force Effectiveness

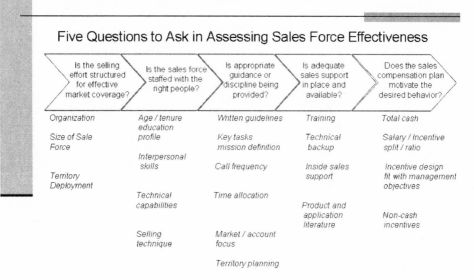

Is the selling effort structured for effective market coverage?	Is the sales force staffed with the right people?	Is appropriate guidance or discipline being provided?	Is adequate sales support in place and available?	Does the sales compensation plan motivate the desired behavior?
Organization	Age / tenure education profile	Written guidelines	Training	Total cash
Size of Sale Force	Interpersonal skills	Key tasks mission definition	Technical backup	Salary / Incentive split / ratio
Territory Deployment	Technical capabilities	Call frequency	Inside sales support	Incentive design fit with management objectives
	Selling technique	Time allocation	Product and application literature	Non-cash incentives
		Market / account focus		
		Territory planning		

Very early in my career (back when the earth was cooling) I was given my very first line-management assignment with Westinghouse Electric Supply, an electrical products distributor. I was relocated from my home state of New York to Chicago, Illinois, where my employer had a significant distribution operation. I was challenged to expand the company's presence in both the industrial and construction markets within this geography. We had a successful organization in place to serve the industrial segment of the market, but the firm had struggled with the construction market for many years. Expanding the industrial sales effort was not terribly difficult, but solving the construction puzzle required considerably more thought.

I quickly assessed that we had previously hired the kinds of sales people that liked to *hang out* with the Chicago contractors, a group known for enjoying the good things that life had to offer. These contractors were primarily interested in acquiring the materials and components they needed to perform their tasks at the lowest possible cost. Our sales associates were doing everything they could to get access to the work these firms were competing for; but at the end of the day, the lowest price prevailed and usually won the business. We had to come up with a different approach, or we would just continue to spin our wheels.

I made a decision to change the makeup of our sales force and hired sales engineers (electrical engineers) instead. This new group of sales associates not only represented our product line more effectively, but they actually knew how our products worked. Instead of sending them out to call on the contractors, I sent them out to call on architectural and engineering firms, the people that actually designed the buildings and recommended the components. Our goal was to become "specified" in the design phase of the construction process because if we could accomplish that, it didn't matter which contractor won the work. They would all need to buy our products.

I am pleased to report that this approach proved to be very successful, and we began to grow our presence within the construction market as a result of this effort. Just selecting a channel and assigning a quota is not the complete answer; understanding how we are going to focus and manage it is equally important. Had I continued to only measure the result (sales against quota), I would not have looked for a way to solve the problem. We want to utilize our channels to reach our targeted customers with our product-positioning message, to provide real time feedback, and to produce the volume of transactions we require to be successful.

Our third objective is to add additional sales channels to accommodate our expansion needs. We will once again use our tree model to help us identify the critical path for accomplishing this objective. We determined in phase 4 of our program that we would need to add (hypothetically) additional channels to insure that we have adequate market coverage. We also indicated that the number of new channels we would need would be determined by the expectations we would assign to each channel. We now have a requirement to add a known number of new sales channels that will be expected to produce an anticipated amount of volume. So, we need to make sure that x number of distributors (or sales people) are contracted, that they have access to product and process training, and that they can support the volume and product requirements we need.

Aligning our sales channels with these targeted customer groups is one of the keys to our success, so making sure that we do this appropriately is critical. The timing of these assignments is going to be driven by the type and complexity of the products we offer. If we are dealing with a technical product requiring a significant direct-sales effort, then we should have this capability in place at least one year in advance of our budgeted revenue cycle. If we are offering a simpler product line via established mass-marketing channels, then this advance time requirement could be shorter. In either event, we will be sure to assign sufficient quotas (sales objectives) to each of these selected channels so that we not only meet our objectives, but also allow for the possibility that some of them could fall short.

If we are utilizing business development personnel as a channel to reach the government markets, then we will need to measure things even differently. We indicated earlier that one of the critical success factors in this market space was our requirement to become part of teaming arrangements that enabled the pursuit of larger government programs. We will want to track the number of teaming partners we have developed relationships with, the number of actual teaming arrangements we are engaged in, and the volume of government programs we are pursuing. We will also track the number of proposals we are part of and the percentage of awards we eventually win. The early indicator here is the number of teams we are part of and the dollar value of the role we will play on these teams as well as our assessment of our ability to enhance the overall team's chances for success.

Our fourth objective is to adequately support our sales efforts by maximizing our advertising and promotion dollars. So, our measurement system has to track whether or not we are spending our dollars in the right places in support of the right things. We already calculated these variables for each of our targeted market segments, and now we want to manage these expenses by product and customer grouping. For example, we may spend less advertising and promotional cost on product X in segment A than we will spend for the same product grouping in segment B. But overall, we are managing the total amount of advertising and promotional cost we will spend for this product grouping as a variable cost element that is measured against the revenues it generates.

Our measurement system also needs to ascertain the effectiveness of our promotional efforts. We are going to require our ad agency to acquire and report feedback on the results from our advertising campaigns. If we are entering a previously uncovered market area and we have undertaken an aggressive awareness campaign, we will want to know how successful that effort was. Advertising agencies are well equipped to provide this kind of feedback for us, and we need to receive this information in a timely manner. We also want the flexibility to alter our current campaigns in the event that we find our efforts to be ineffective. We will want to move the dollars and effort from one segment to another market or product segment if we discover a need to do so.

In our hypothetical example, 10 percent of our revenues have been allocated to manage our total marketing mix costs. Thirty percent of this allocation (3 percent of budgeted revenues) was assigned to support our advertising and promotion efforts, and this expenditure is managed by those of us within the marketing function. We want to spend these dollars in a way that provides the most benefit, so we need to track it very carefully. We must make sure that our ad agency reports their expenditures in a format that matches our campaigns, and that our accounting group records these costs in the similar manner. We have to have the flexibility to move promotional dollars from one campaign to another or from one market segment to another, depending on the tactics we may have to change.

We will establish a set of requirements with our advertising agency that identifies each of our specific campaigns and the cost we expect to incur in implementing these campaigns. We will also document the timelines in which we can expect feedback from these efforts. This set of matrices will help us to monitor not only the cost we incur by market segment, but the impact we are having by market segment. If we have a promotion campaign in progress to support a channel that is not handling our volume requirements, we want to identify this circumstance as early as possible so that we can reallocate these funds elsewhere. We will monitor these expense categories in the total as well, just to be sure that in the execution of our plans we do not exceed the total amount allocated for these purposes. This will be the comparison others will be watching.

Our fifth objective was to be sure that we managed our channels and promotional expenditures within our budgeted guidelines. We will receive our monthly operating statement from the CFO, but it will most likely report these expenditures in the aggregate unless we ask for it differently. What we want to know is how much we are spending by targeted market segment for these activities and then want to compare the actual costs we are incurring to the results we are achieving. Remember, we only have an allocated amount to spend (hypothetically 5 percent of revenues for channels, 3 percent of revenues for promotion). If we are spending these dollars in category A and need to move them to category B, we have to be able to track this expense shift.

Our measurement system has to provide us with monthly reports that track these expenditures in this format. We want to know exactly how much each channel is costing us each month and then compare it to the cost estimate we derived from our mother of all matrices. We also need to know the sales volume each of these channels is generating so that we can compare their contribution to the cost we incur. It is a very rewarding experience to discover that a channel is costing more than we had planned because they are producing more than we expected. As long as the cost is in proportion to the contribution, we do not have an expense management issue. Our measurement system needs to insure that we see these items in this same relationship format.

Our sixth objective was to realize our product plan assumptions, and our product managers will have to assemble several pieces of essential data for us to review. We are going to want to know how we are progressing in terms of units and dollars. How many units of product groups—A, B, C, and D—did we sell within each time period, and how does that compare to our product plan assumptions? They will need to provide us with the number of units sold, revenues per product grouping, as well as any pricing anomalies we may have discovered. We will also want to know the related direct costs incurred to produce them and the resulting gross margins they generated.

Tracking our product performance is important for a number of reasons. First of all, we have all of the production and supply-chain implications to recognize. Secondly, we have the related impacts on our planned marketing mix, how we assigned channel expectations and allocated promotion costs. And third, we have to consider their potential impacts on revenue growth and market share gain. We can only achieve our targeted growth objective by selling a planned number of units at an expected price to a targeted group of potential customers. If we cannot realize these product volumes, then we have to look at other possible remedies such as additional promotional efforts or possible price concessions. If we do not track these variations at the individual product level, we will not know where our problems exist.

In addition to just tracking the total number of units we are selling in the aggregate, we want to know which set of targeted customers is buying which set of products. This is important to know because it measures the very foundation of our market planning assumptions. We believed that we could sell a certain volume of product to a certain set of targeted customers, and if the demand is not there, we have to adjust. This may require us to sell more of this same product to a different customer group or adjust our expectations for this product line and offset it with additional sales of other product offerings.

We should also solicit feedback with respect to our customer's satisfaction with our products and our company's support of these products. If we are utilizing a direct-sales channel to reach our targeted customers, then their reports can include this kind of information. If we are using indirect channels to reach our customers, then warranty registrations can be structured to include product experience or satisfaction requests. We need to receive, collate, and respond to any dissatisfaction patterns we recognize within this information.

Our seventh objective was to introduce new product offerings, so we will want an early feedback system that reports our progress for new product development. As part of our product planning process, we constructed a project plan for each of the new products we expect to introduce throughout the planning period. Each project plan contains specific milestones and timelines that enabled the accomplishment of each stage of the process. Regularly reviewing these individual project plans and evaluating their progress is our measurement tool. We can coordinate our actual progress with our planned introductory timelines and discover any risk factors we need to consider.

Our product development model provides for seven distinct decision points at each stage gate of the process. We should be able to anticipate which new product concepts we are going to abandon and which ones we are going to continue with by stage 3 of the process. This will be our early indicator, and it provides us with early insight into the viability of our new product planning assumptions. Once these first three hurdles are cleared, we will discover in stage 4 of the process whether or not we can produce these products within our expected time frames and at the cost points we anticipated. In stages 5 and 6, we will know what our production plans will be and have a sense of when we can actually trial these new products and test market their application. At stage seven, we will be ready to introduce them and track their acceptance.

If we should find ourselves struggling during this introductory stage, we have to quickly determine if it is due to pricing, features, or the way we have positioned and promoted our new offering. We have convinced the organization to invest in the development of these new products, so we have to pay very close attention to their market acceptance. Our revenue plan was predicated on the availability of new products at a given moment in time, and the successful attainment of our plan is dependent on this critical factor. Should we find ourselves delayed or find that the introduction is taking hold slower than we predicted, we will need to adjust somewhere else within our marketing mix. Again, the earlier we can make these determinations, the better our chance to react in time and seek alternatives.

Our eighth objective was to generate a required amount of revenues and margin as the result of our product sales. We want to measure and manage the available gross margin we generate from each of our targeted market segments. The available gross margin is the sale price of an item, less the direct cost of producing that item, less any variable cost associated with selling and promoting that item, less any other additional variable expenses, such as warranty, bad debt, and inventory obsolescence. We want to know what this calculation is by targeted market segment so that if any one of our variable cost elements (the ones we can control) begins to negatively impact our expected contribution margin, we can make adjustments.

Calculating Available Gross Margin

ITEM		UNIT PRICE
Net Sales	100%	$ 100.00
Direct Cost of Goods	60%	$ 60.00
Gross Margin	40%	$ 40.00
Variable Expenses		
Commissions (Channel)	5.0%	$ 5.00
Advertising & Promotion	3.0%	$ 3.00
Delivery	1.5%	$ 1.50
Freight In	1.0%	$ 1.00
Warranty Provision	2.0%	$ 2.00
Bad Debt Provision	0.5%	$ .50
Inventory Obsolescence	0.5%	$ .50
	13.5%	$ 13.50
Available Gross Margin	**26.5%**	**$ 26.50**

We now have visibility at the contribution level for our tactical choices because we know the available gross margin that each group of targeted customers is expected to provide. Our revenue projections, product sales, support costs, and distribution costs are now aligned with and measured against how well they serve our targeted customer groups. If we find ourselves falling short of our projections, we can adjust our advertising and promotional costs, consolidate our fulfillment and support structures, change our warranty policy, realign our distribution channels, etc. We are going to construct virtual P&Ls (profit and loss statements) for each of these targeted groups that include revenues, direct costs, gross margins, and all the other marketing costs so that we can measure the available gross margin each contributes.

The one factor that always has an impact on the outcome of our margin expectations is product pricing. Price pressure is a reality of the competitive world and somewhere within our execution phase we will be compelled to consider price adjustments that we hadn't planned on. What we must be aware of is the impact of these price changes when we make them, and the offsets that would be required to adjust for them. If there is a decline in gross margin, it is going to change the amount of revenues required to cover our planned expenses. We have to know what this impact would be in advance of making these pricing decisions.

Establishing Market Segment P&Ls

	Market Segment A Budgeted	Market Segment A Actual	Variance Report
Revenues	$3,000,000	$3,250,000	$250,000
Direct Costs	$2,250,000	$2,450,000	$200,000
Gross Margin	$ 750,000	$ 800,000	$50,000
Channel Cost	$150,000	$160,000	$10,000
Promotion	$90,000	$85,000	($ 5,000)
Allocations	$60,000	$60,000	$ 0
Contribution	$450,000	$ 495,000	$45,000

In our hypothetical example, at $10 million of revenues the loss of 1 percent of our forecasted 10 percent available gross margin would reduce our expected margins by $100,000. In order to cover our projected fixed expenses of $500,000, we would have to increase our *breakeven revenues* from $5 million to $6.66 million. We would have to sell an additional $1.66 million at the lower price point just to earn enough margin to cover our fixed costs. So if we agree to lower our price, we need to determine whether or not we can benefit from new incremental sales volumes to offset the margin loss.

We can also return to our mother of all matrices and look for ways to readdress our variable cost assumptions and make expense adjustments. Changing our pricing, volumes, mix, etc., within this model will help us to understand what these different impacts are in depth. It will also provide us with a format to explore other options within our marketing mix to offset this circumstance.

Our ninth goal was to utilize cost effective logistics for the fulfillment and support of our offerings. In phase 3 of our program, when we selected our targeted customers, we tried to take into consideration their location or geography. We took the information we learned from this exercise and plotted it onto a map so that we could find areas where our target customers were clustered, areas where we could serve them from a single, rather than multiple locations. This also enabled us to consider these same locales as places where we could open or close regional and local offices in support of our sales efforts. So, we need to determine whether or not we met these changing infrastructure requirements.

Estimating Impact of Margin Loss

Line Category	Budget or Plan	Revised Forecast
Fixed Expenses	$ 500,000	$ 500,000
Available Gross Margin	10%	09%
Annual Breakeven Point	$ 5,000,000	$ 6,666,666
Annual Profits	$ 500,000	$ 500,000

Use Breakeven formula and the incremental profit required

$$\frac{\text{Fixed Expenses + Lost Profit}}{\text{Available Gross Margin}} = \text{New Breakeven Point}$$

$$\frac{\$500,000 + \$100,000}{.09} = \mathbf{\$6,666,666}. \text{ or } \underline{\mathbf{\$1,666,666}} \text{ Additional Sales !}$$

If our organization has a separate group that handles facilities, then we need to formalize plans with this group to accommodate our forecasted needs. It is in everyone's best interest if we can find a way to collocate with other parts of the organization as it helps to control costs. There are additional good customer-relationship reasons to collocate the channel management effort with warehousing and shipping. It improves cross-functional communication and enables the accurate conveyance of delivery information to the ultimate customer. It can also result in a more collaborative working environment for all of the stakeholders, so we need to ensure the establishment of these facilities in response to the requirements of our plan.

If our organization does not have a group that handles these kinds of requirements, then we are going to have to establish these facilities on our own. Once again we will use our tree model to insure that we track all of the necessary steps within the required time frames. Locales have to be decided, alternative facilities need to be compared, and leases need to be negotiated and signed. Furniture and equipment need to be purchased and delivered, communications systems installed, and local area networks established to accommodate data processing needs. We are once again tracking the completion of the required steps needed to accomplish our goal, establishing a regional facility to support our market and product plans.

Our tenth objective is to win the game in the marketplace and aggressively grow our business 27 percent or more per annum. We are now measuring our topline progress from multiple points of view. We are measuring sales volumes by revenues per customer, customer group, and market segment. We are measuring sales volumes by product offering and units sold. We are measuring the impact of our new product introductions in a similar manner, only paying much closer attention to each phase of their early development and introduction. We are now sensitized to pricing and promotional costs and can trace the impact of these choices directly to product volume and to customer group purchases. So if we are off in our assumptions and projections, we should be able to isolate where the shortfall is and have an opportunity to take corrective action.

Our CFO's team will provide us with monthly operating statements that will report actual revenues versus the budget we submitted in phase 5 of our program. We need to receive this information monthly in as timely a fashion that is practical. Although this report is a reflection of what has already occurred, it is the official record of our organization, and we need to be prepared to address any significant variances. Revenues are generated from the successful presentation of our products and services to the targeted customers we have identified. Once an order was received, we processed its requirements and insured that it was fulfilled and delivered. If we pay attention to all of the things we identified via our tree model for execution, then these numbers should start to take care of themselves.

Our eleventh goal is to double our market share over the course of five years from 10 to 20 percent. To insure that we are on the right track, we need to validate our market plan with the information we currently have, and then test our assumptions annually. We know from phase 1 of the program that our industry is expected to grow at 10 percent per annum over the course of the next five years. We know from the market plan we just developed in phase 5 of the program that for us to double our market share, we would need to grow at 27 percent or more per annum. This requires us (in our hypothetical example) to grow our revenues from $10 million today to $32 million in year five. So if we accomplish this, does it produce the result we are trying to achieve?

We can validate our market plan direction by comparing what we have planned to accomplish to what we believe the rest of the industry will be like. Although we can never be sure of the reactions and plans of our competitors, we can make the assumption that if things continued as before, we should accomplish our objective. We calculate this comparison by projecting our business-as-usual position (10-percent share for the next five years) and then contrasting it to our current plans (20-percent share in year five). When we add it all up, it should tell us whether or not our plans are aligned with our goals. It can also tell us whether or not we will benefit as a result of this effort because there will most likely be some early cost incurred before the full benefit of our plans are realized.

Validating the Market Plan

Category	Yr. 1	Yr. 2	Yr. 3	Yr. 4	Yr. 5
Budgeted Growth (27%)	$12.7M	$16.3M	$20.5M	$26.0M	$32.0M
Industry Growth (10%)	$11.0M	$12.1M	$13.3M	$14.6M	$16.10M
Incremental Revenues	$ 1.7M	$4.2M	$7.2M	$11.4M	$15.9M
Direct Cost of Goods (75%)	$1.2M	$3.1M	$5.4M	$8.5M	$11.9M
Contribution Margin (25%)	$0.5M	$1.1M	$1.8M	$2.9M	$4.0M
Incremental Est. Cost	$.5	$.7	$.9	$1.1	$1.3
Incremental Benefit	$0.0M	$0.4M	$0.9M	$1.8M	$3.7M

Our twelfth and final goal is to improve our ranking within the industry. Since we are not the determinant of these rankings, it would be difficult for us to devise a measurement system that supports its achievement. But we can, and will, devise a feedback system in phase 7 of the program to help us track these perceptions. In addition to a revenue ranking, we will want to remain cognizant of the other influences that go into making these determinations. Product quality and customer relationships are two areas that we can measure that will most likely be factors that effect our position.

Quality assurance can be measured in a number of ways, from very specific statistical quality control practices, to the resulting customer reaction to our efforts. Service levels are another perceived quality factor, as well as standardized business practices for customer care. *Customer Relationship Magazine* recently published a list of best practices for sustaining customer satisfaction and suggested we pay attention to the following:

Ease of customer access or availability
Actual order and service response times

Product and service quality
Overall customer perception

In addition to direct customer feedback, there are other commercial relationships that define the kind of company we are, so our handling of credit issues, billing and settlements, and vendor relationships can also impact our industry ranking.

The most difficult area to measure objectively is overall customer satisfaction, as beauty and performance are all in the eyes of the beholder. We do know that customer dissatisfaction is a very real deterrent to repeat or follow on sales, so we need to make an effort to understand potential customer concerns. The major categories of customer dissatisfaction are as follows:

Prepurchase advertising that represents a product as something different than what it actually is

Purchase transactions that did not complete satisfactorily for delivery, etc.

Product performance that did not meet industry standards (guarantee, warranty, or contract terms and conditions that were different than what was believed to have been agreed to)

Service or repair experience that was difficult to obtain

Transaction practices such as deposit/credit/collection that was not administered in a courteous or professional manner

We will select a reputable publication (or two) to benchmark our industry position and then track it on a regular basis. When we construct our management reports, we will include any changes within these rankings. We will develop and implement measurement matrices to address the four customer care areas identified above as a starting point. As we discover other elements for consideration, we will add them to our internal performance indicators. Whatever is important to our customer is important to us, and we need to measure and implement these KPIs, (key performance indicators) and SLAs, (service level agreements) throughout our supply chain, channel agreements, and internal organization.

The critical path to achieving our goals includes the assurance of a sustainable supply of quality-checked product units, available in the quantities we require necessary to achieve our revenue plans. These products need to be represented by capable sales channels and supported by adequate logistics to enable their timely delivery. Our products need to be priced competitively, consistent with the parameters we set forth in our original product plans and supported on a market segment by market-segment basis with the appropriate amount of advertising and promotion. Our measurement systems need to track all of the critical paths we are on and provide us with the earliest signs of variations from plan as practical.

Our measurement indices are going to look different from company to company, but it is important to understand the concept of aligning our data points with the earliest known activities that influence the outcome of our plans. It is equally important to align the contractual agreements we enter into with others to drive the desired behaviors we want in support of our goals and objectives. If we have specific quality-assurance requirements to meet in the delivery of our products and services, then these provisions need to be understood throughout the whole supply chain. If we have critical time commitments to meet as part of our delivery process, then these conditions need to be understood throughout the order entry and fulfillment process.

Once again we can relate to our field commander as he or she enters the battlefield. We know our environment; we know our competitive landscape; we know what markets and customers we have targeted; we know what products and services we have to go to market with; we have aligned our channels; we have quantified our market objectives and focused our resources. We have just devised and implemented a measurement system (governance model) that will help us to measure our progress along each of our critical paths (battle fronts) on a real-time basis. We are now engaged.

Phase 6 Deliverables

We begin establishing our governance model by collaborating with the financial control function within our organization to populate the operating statement with the market plan we have adopted. The totals should be comprised of the individual product sales, by unit, for each of these accounting periods, and the associated direct costs should be accounted for in the same way.

Sources of information:

> Our market plan and resulting revenue plan
> Our product plans and new product introduction plans
> Our established pricing and current cost estimates

We will next establish our departmental or functional operating budget for the activities we will provide in support of the marketing mix. We will be compliant with the operating-statement categories provided by the financial and control group, and align our projected costs by salaries, travel and entertainment expenses, facilities and support costs, and all outside contracted services.

Sources of information:

> Our resource plans as determined in phase 5
> Our planned expenditures for advertising and promotion
> Our planned expenditures for channel costs

We will next begin to assemble the information we need to track to measure our product plan. We constructed product-positioning matrices as part of our product-planning effort and made certain assumptions about how we could price our offerings.

These price points have been loaded into our budgets as they are the foundation for our revenue projections.

Sources of information:

> Our product and pricing plans
> Actual sales transactions
> Competitive response

We want to track our channel activities and determine whether or not they are contacting our targeted customers and introducing our products and services. We assigned specific targets and volume expectations to each of these channels, so we want to measure their progress toward accomplishing our objectives. We need for them to provide weekly activity and sales reports so that we can measure the effectiveness of the choices we made.

Sources of information:

> Channel-sales activity reports
> Contracted sales made by each of the respective channels (new sales)
> Backlog of sales made by each of the respective sales channels (orders
>   in house)

We want to continue to populate our customer database with the things we are learning about each of our targeted customers as part of this effort. For example, should we learn that one of our targeted accounts is currently obligated under an existing contract to purchase our competitors products until some date in the future, we will want to document this. We would want to make sure that our sales efforts intensify in advance of this expiration date so that we have an opportunity to garner the next contract.

Sources of information:

> Sales activity reports
> Customer database

We also want to establish our own set of contribution models to measure our effectiveness by market segment. For this we need the help of the accountants once again, and they need to create a management accounting system that mirrors the operating statement of the firm for each of the segments we want to track. We are going to measure revenues, products sold, direct costs, channel costs, and promotional costs on a segment-by-segment basis to understand the real cost and value of serving these targeted segments of the market.

Sources of information:

> Company's operating statement
> Our product plan from the mother of all matrices
> Our allocation of advertising and promotional costs
> Our actual contract terms for each of the channels we have assigned
> All other applicable marketing-mix costs of serving these market segments

The purpose of phase 6 of our program has been to develop a set of operating measurements that can be relied on to govern the success of our market plan. We want to look beyond the reported results and identify and measure those activities that drive the business. We know that in order to succeed, we have to accomplish a specific set of tasks, in an organized fashion, within a given time frame, with a defined quantity of resources. Tracking these elements as early as possible in the process enables us to make any necessary adjustments along the way.

Checklist

Operating statement populated with revenue plan
Operating statement populated with product plan
Operating statement populated with marketing expenses
New product stage-gate development plans and separate budget
Channel quota assignments and compensation models
Channel sales activity reporting process and feedback loops
Advertising and promotion campaign tracking reports
Product-plan-variation reports to track pricing and volume
Virtual P&L statements by market segments to measure our progress on
    a market-by-market basis

PHASE 7

Feedback

The fastest way to succeed is to look as if you're playing by other peoples rules, while quietly playing by your own.

—Michael Korda

It is now time to execute our plans, measure our progress, and solicit the feedback we need to enable us to determine whether or not we have made the right choices. Our goal at this stage of the program is to develop feedback mechanisms that will allow us to evaluate our progress on three fronts: the quantitative measurements we established in phase 5 and 6; the critical paths we established in phase 6; and external perception of those who gather and track information about our industry and our company. We can track and evaluate the internal measurements and milestones we developed on our own, but we cannot qualify customer or industry perception independently.

Whatever the universe is that we compete in, we will need feedback. We must have a plan to receive and analyze this constant stream of changing information so that we can make adjustments. This final segment of our plan needs to consider the following:

> The milestone reporting we seek from our operating teams with respect to the critical paths we have developed for implementation
>
> The profit-and-loss statements generated by the financial reporting group and the variance reports we will be asked to provide.
>
> The market segment reports that portray the available gross margin and contribution realized from our marketing-mix selections

The monthly variance reports from our product management function portraying our actual to planned progress for our product plans

The stage-gate reporting we have established for our product development plans and the critical decision points

The professional associations whose members form opinions about our products, services, and technology choices

The financial analyst who tracks our industry and influence the opinions of others with respect to our industry position and marketing effectiveness

The quality/customer satisfaction surveyors who pronounce a "best" or "best in class" opinion for the products and services we have to offer

The published reports that stack rank companies, products, and services based on independent survey data they collect

The very first thing we should always recognize in acquiring feedback is the purpose for it, why the information is being solicited to begin with. Our intent in this phase of our program is to use the feedback we receive to make the necessary course corrections to implementing our market plans. When pilots take off from an airport, they have full fuel tanks that deplete over the course of their flight. They adjust the ailerons on the plane throughout the flight to account for this constant shift in weight. If they did not make these adjustments, the aircraft would lose its equilibrium and potentially crash. We want to be able to make the required adjustments along our journey as well so that we get to where we want to go without crashing.

Financial Reporting

We are going to be receiving the traditional financial reports from our accounting function. The company's formal operating statement will provide us with revenues, cost of goods sold, gross margins, and operating costs. This will be the indicator of our overall financial performance against the quantitative objectives we set for ourselves in phases 4 and 5. We also have a need to determine which products have been selling and which ones are lagging behind, so we will want a report that provides information about our product revenues in terms of units sold and dollars generated.

We should also be receiving an accounting of our expenses and a comparison of the amounts we are spending to the budget we established for these costs. We have requested that these expenses be broken down further and attributed to each of the market segments we have established. We need this information so that we can track the impact of our channel costs and advertising and promotion expenditures by market segment. We want the ability to monitor and reallocate these expenses in this fashion as part of our governance process.

The other financial report we requested was for virtual profit and loss statements for each of the market segments we established. We are asking to have revenues, cost of goods sold, gross margins, advertising and promotion costs, channel costs, and other identified expenses, attributed to each of these segments. What we want to determine is whether or not the market planning assumptions we made for each of these market segments is coming to fruition or not. If we expect to be growing at 20 percent in segment A and 30 percent in segment B and discover that we are not, we need to understand why. Once we determine the root cause of any variance, we will have to make adjustments.

The other valuable element to the financial reports we will receive is visibility into our total operating costs and how these dollars are being spent. We asked for the ability to move expenditures from one market segment to another to accommodate changes in market conditions and priorities. What we do not want to do is lose sight of what we are spending in total, so having a roll up of these expenses helps us to manage these items. The formal operating statement will report these costs in the aggregate, but we will be managing them by market segment and product groups. Knowing the aggregate of these expenditures helps us to keep these costs under control.

All financial reports reflect what has already occurred, but that does not mean that they can't be used to forecast the future. For example, if we have initiated a promotional campaign to launch a new product in various segments of the market, we are not going to know the success of that campaign for several months. But we can begin to recognize the early indicators from the campaign by paying attention to our incremental new orders and our growing backlog. Our financial reports communicate these early indicators to us, and this information provides quantitative insight into things to come. All of these financial reports provide useful feedback for us, and they are an important tool for us to use in the administration of our responsibilities.

Key financial indicators to pay close attention to are
 new orders received, sales;
 unshipped orders in house, backlog;
 recognized revenues, orders shipped;
 returns, allowances, discounts;
 cost of goods sold;

reported gross margins;
market segment contributions;
product plan variations;
channel cost in relationship to volume generated;
advertising and promotion costs in relationship to campaigns; and
departmental expenditures.

Just tracking these financial scorecards of the company does not insure that the right things are happening within the organization. To achieve our aggressive growth objective, several major adjustments needed to be made to our current marketing mix, and we are changing to a new way of managing this marketing mix. If all we track is the "business-as-usual result indicators, we won't know whether or not the required changes ever took place within our organization. We need to add another dimension to our feedback process to provide visibility into these change areas to help us achieve our desired results.

Critical-path Feedback

In phase 6 of the program, we listed several hypothetical critical paths that needed to be followed for us to implement our growth plans. We suggested that we adopt a similar approach to developing these paths that a program manager takes to organize a large project. In other words, what are the activities that we identified to be accomplished and within what time frames do they need to occur? For example, we determined that we had to add additional sales channels or direct sales personnel to grow our customer base. Who is responsible for getting that accomplished and by when does it have to be completed? Our financial reporting systems cannot address these kinds of issues.

What we have to do is build a feedback mechanism to report our progress along each of the critical paths we developed in phase 6. We used our tree model to link each of the major milestones we want to accomplish, and now we have to transfer this information into a measurable format for us to track. For example, if we did not contract with the new distribution channels, establish the correct service level agreements, integrate our business practices, and agree on volume commitments, etc., nothing is going to happen differently. If nothing happens differently, then we are not going to garner the new customers we are seeking, and we are not going to grow the business at an accelerated rate.

These are the levers and gauges we want to measure and manage, as these are the early indicators that influence the outcome of our plans. We have to establish a communication system between our channels and ourselves so that we can track their efforts toward reaching our goals. If we do not set up the business reporting processes, we cannot possibly know whether they are reaching our targeted customers or not. We also want to be able to obtain sales-forecast information, relevant customer feedback, etc. If no one sets up the process to collect this information, then the feedback systems will never be there. We could risk everything we are trying to accomplish by not following through on these critical tasks.

We (hypothetically) identified ten different critical paths we had to create and measure in the last phase of the program. We now want to capture the essence of these items in a format that enables us to garner feedback about our progress toward achieving these milestones. We will need to create what engineers and project managers call a Gantt chart, a linear representation of these events and timelines. We will copy our tree model to develop these charts because all of the tasks we need to accomplish have already been identified within these models. The desired result taken from each of our tree models will become our major project task. Milestones are then transferred from the first set of tree branches and subsequent tasks from the next set of branches of the tree. We now set the timelines for the completion of these tasks and link together any related or dependent activities.

Critical Path Feedback

Timeline	Month 1	Month 2	Month 3	etc
Goal 1				
Milestone A				
Task a				
Task b				
Milestone B				
Task a				
Goal 2				
Milestone A				
Task a				
Task b				
Milestone B				
Task a				

If we should discover that we are unable to accomplish an identified task, then we need to quickly assess what our alternatives could be. What we do not want to occur is the infamous surprise, discovering an implementation problem after the financial reports have already reported our shortcomings. All that any of us can do is the best we can; but if we neglected to establish the necessary distribution channels, didn't make the efforts to integrate the required business practices, or inappropriately managed expectations, shame on us. We have to track the activities that drive the results to make sure that they are occurring within the time frames they need to occur. Remember, the earlier in the process we can recognize a problem, the higher the probability is that we can correct it or find an alternative.

Customer Feedback

In 1988, Learning Dynamics Inc. conducted a customer commitment survey. A total of 180 managers responded from eighty-six different companies to report on the quality of service within the United States. Seventy-five percent of the respondents agreed that service quality in the United States was not very good, and they either rated it as fair or poor.

The survey results reflect why.

Only 57 percent rate "meeting customer needs" as their number one priority.

In 62 percent of the companies, not everyone is aware of what customers do with the product or service they offer.

Fewer than half of the new products or services developed or improved were based on customer suggestions or complaints, despite an MIT study showing that the best innovations come from customers

Only 59 percent of the respondents contact lost customers; 7 percent did nothing when they lost a customer

In some companies (17 percent), not even salespeople actually talk to customers. It gets worse for senior management. Twenty-two percent don't talk to them; marketing, 29 percent; and research and development, 67 percent. Only 60 percent report they base their competitive strategy primarily on attention to customer needs. What is ironic is that 21 percent claim to base competitive strategy on product quality, but the only way to define *quality* is to ask customers

Thirty-three percent claim their marketing strategy aims to produce business from new, as opposed to repeat customers. This strategy is only viable for the funeral home business as companies are usually better off cultivating their existing customers

Assimilating customer feedback requires us to visit with customers, distributors, wholesalers, and potential users and hear what they have to say about our products and services. What they liked, what we need to improve, and where we stand in relationship to other alternatives that they may be considering. What we are looking for in this process are patterns, common perceptions, things that will enable us to make corrections and adjustments to the way we are serving their needs. This is without a doubt the most important feedback we need to receive!

There are other methods for acquiring customer feedback, and conducting user—or focus-group sessions is another approach. These groups should be assembled to represent a cross section of our targeted customer segments and be conducted in an open manner. There can be valuable information attained in these forums, and a list of priorities for product improvement can evolve from these sessions. If the majority of the group is relatively satisfied, then we can assume we are on the right track. Conversely, if the majority of the group feels uncomfortable about a particular issue, then it is in our best interests to address it.

We do not want to overlook any independent research we may be systematically collecting on our own. In phase 1 of the program, we discussed utilizing a research firm to help us develop our original market and industry assumptions. When we conduct this research in a follow-on manner, we can obtain additional feedback as to whether or not our planning assumptions have been proven to be correct. This research can be updated to survey industry perceptions, product acceptance, or specific business practices we were attempting to implement. The value of this approach is that we can compare the later acquired results to our original set of norms and measure any changes in customer perception.

Other sources for customer feedback are industry forums, professional associations, and trade shows. Here is a chance to observe what customer's think of our competitors, and talk informally with potential new customers. These events are attended by wholesalers and distributors, buyers and sellers, and usually covered by industry and trade publications. What we are looking for in this environment is recognition of our intensified marketing efforts. We also need to be aware of the impact that our programs are having on our competitions and pay close attention to their reactions.

Product Feedback

When we begin to look for feedback on our individual product offerings, we will find a plethora of choices to consider in this area as well. When we go to the Consumer Reports Web site (www.consumerreports.org) we quickly discover that they have an opinion on three thousand or more categories of consumer wares. They have recorded "expert test results" on thousands of products and have correlated these results into various product rankings and opinions. This fact of life presents the familiar good—and bad-news scenario. The good news is that this comparison becomes an easily attainable data point for us to acquire. The bad news is it is also a very easy data point for others to acquire, so if there should be an unfavorable report, others will readily know about it. If we are producing a consumer product, this kind of information is going to be out there, and we need to pay attention to it.

When we went to acquire industrial product comparisons, there was no shortage of places to look either. These kinds of comparisons are classified by industry and industrial product groupings (software, hardware, adhesives, power tools, motors, etc.). The current marketing tactic being utilized to differentiate products in this community is independent testing laboratories to document comparisons. Manufacturers and producers submit their products to these labs who in turn certify that they are what they say they are, and then they compare them to other similar products. The most familiar of these test labs is Underwriter's Laboratories, who sets performance standards and issues a seal of approval that warrants the attributes of a product. These tests are often conducted in parallel with other industry participants, and the results are published in industry and trade journals.

If our product is sent to an independent laboratory for testing, and they inform us of potential defects, we may need to redesign the product to correct these deficiencies. If we discover that we are noncompliant with an established industry standard (ISO) or our customer considers this to be a qualifying consideration, then we need to correct that problem. If we discover that our product quality is ranked last by a credible survey organization (e.g., J. D. Powers) then we need go back and visit our quality-control and quality-assurance processes. Organizing a feedback system is all about being able to recognize a need for change and then responding to that need in a fashion that allows the organization to make corrections and progress.

Third-party surveys are continuing to gain greater credibility in today's marketplace, and paying attention to this trend is important. If our products and services fall into a category that is under constant vigilance from one of these quality assurance organizations, then their opinions of us and our products will influence our customer's choices. It is best to get to know these groups—understand their survey methodology, the questions they ask, and the groups they target—to make sure that we have a campaign of our own to address these same concerns.

I shared with you earlier in the manuscript that I spent a good portion of my career with US West, one of the Regional Bell Operating Companies. After having successfully transitioned the federal government market unit, I was reminded that no good deed goes unpunished in corporate America, and I was provided with a new challenge. My next challenging assignment was to lead the business and government services market unit, which consisted of my original federal government market unit, plus the state and local government market unit, and our large business services unit. Although the buying characteristics of these groups were notably different, the applications and services they required were very, very similar.

Shortly into this new assignment, I was introduced to one of our largest commercial customers, Motorola. At the time, Motorola was led by Bob Galvin, the originator and evangelist for Sigma 6, Motorola's industry-leading quality performance standard. Mr. Galvin made it very clear that all of the suppliers to Motorola had to meet this quality threshold, or Motorola would not allow them to be part of Motorola's supply chain. I foolishly tried to imitate Lily Tomlin and explain that "we were the phone company" and that these kinds of things didn't apply to us. Boy was I wrong! Motorola made it very clear that if we wouldn't guarantee the performance of our services to the Sigma 6 quality level, that they would find somebody else to handle their communication requirements. Ouch!

Explaining this new requirement to our network operations group was not the most popular of undertakings. There is a great deal of pride and tradition within these engineering ranks (after all, according to them they invented the business), and the thought of some outsider telling them what they needed to do was hard for them to digest. But if Motorola did not have an alternative choice today, they would certainly have one tomorrow, and if we couldn't upgrade and guarantee the quality of the services we provided, some other firm would be happy to replace us. We eventually found a way to meet this new requirement and developed a series of SLAs (service level agreements) with Motorola that met the Sigma 6 standards, and US West (now Qwest) has been enjoying their continued support ever since.

Unless we are so small that we are below the radar of these kinds of groups, somewhere there will be a comparison of our products and services to our competitors; and opinions will be formed from the information these groups publish and provide. As the marketing practitioners for our organizations, we must not only pay attention to the things going on within our own sphere of influence, but also those things that impact that sphere of influence. If we are not paying attention to these opinions in the marketplace, then we will fall short of our objectives. But if we are paying attention to them, we can usually find another approach, adjust our product plans to match our competition, and make ourselves more attractive to the ultimate buyer.

Third-party Feedback

Trade publications are another good source of feedback because they keep track of all of the industry's comings and goings and offer opinions as to how we all relate to one another. Some of this should be to be taken with a grain of salt as good press is not always good information. Large industry players will often use this medium as a way to introduce future products and services and throw their competition off guard with these announcements. But if the trade press feels strong enough to print an article about something, there is usually a basis for that decision. We need to pay attention to what these publishers are saying about us and our competitor's activities.

Specific industry associations are another source of feedback that we need to pay attention to. These industry associations compile and correlate operating data and distribute it back to the association's members. The value of this is that all of the members can benefit from knowing what the industry norms are and how they fare in relationship to other industry participants of comparable size. Boards will often tie senior management compensation to the results of these industry surveys, seeking to sustain a position at the top of a particular industry or industry segment.

Stakeholder Perception

When we are looking for third-party feedback, we cannot forget to include the financial community. This group has the opportunity to track and compare any number of organizations across any number of industries. They traditionally assign specific analyst to specific industries, and these individuals, over time, become extremely knowledgeable about how the companies they are following operate. They will rank these companies according to their rules and will not be shy about providing an opinion as to how well they are being managed. Needless to say, the C crowd pays a great deal of attention to this information and will often use this as the influence to effect changes in strategy and direction for the firm.

There are other types of stakeholder comparisons being made by groups such as the American Consumer Satisfaction Index (www.theacsi.org) and the Customer Satisfaction Measurement Association (www.csmassociation.org). These groups benchmark different organizations in relationship to customer satisfaction surveys they conduct, and they do publish their results. The ACSI organization conducts these surveys on behalf of the federal government and reports their findings to the Government Accountability Office and Congress. The CSM Association currently has over three thousand members and participants and reports on the automobile supply industry, financial services, government services, healthcare, information technology, insurance, pharmaceuticals, telecommunications, and utilities.

And finally, we want to make sure that we are measuring our own progress toward attaining our stated industry goal for the enterprise. We wanted to improve our industry ranking from our starting position (validated by a credible industry source) to our desired position (the improved position we are striving to achieve). We must make sure that we are receiving the latest publications from this source and tracking our progress toward this objective.

So here we are, once again in a comparable position to our field commander. We are now actively engaged in the execution of our plans, we are watching all of our key indicators, and we are receiving continuous feedback from our forward observers with respect to our progress. We have done all we can do to plan for the successful achievement of our objectives and should feel confident that if we follow the critical path we have outlined for ourselves, it should lead to the outcome we want to achieve. We will now follow the proven quality assurance model to manage our execution: plan (which we have now completed); do (implementing the tasks along our critical paths); check (paying attention to our progress and measurement reports); act (adjusting to the feedback we receive as required).

Phase 7 Deliverables

We are going to want to receive the organization's operating statements on a monthly basis with a comparison of actual to budgeted performance for each of the categories affected by our efforts. Revenues cost of goods sold, gross margin, related expenses, etc.

Sources of information:

Accounting and finance group

In addition to the traditional statements, we are going to want to see our virtual profit and loss statements for each of the market segments we have targeted reflecting these related operating costs and contribution.

Sources of information:

> Accounting and finance group

We are going to require a monthly variance report for our product plan comparing units and dollars sold to our original assumptions to enable us to manage production forecasts, inventory, etc.

Sources of information:

> Accounting and finance group
> Product management group

We are going to want to receive weekly reports on the specific implementation plans that we have developed for each of our critical path activities. We need to know as early as possible if we are achieving the things we need to accomplish in support of our market plan.

Sources of information:

> Marketing staff
> Operations personnel
> Customer care
> Information processing

We are going to want to receive summaries of the periodicals we identified in our planning process as important sources of industry perception. We are seeking to track our ranking within our industry as well as any feedback issues that could effect our market position.

Source of Information:

> Industry and professional associations
> Trade magazines and publications

Investment banking community
Industry and trade associations

We want to be sure that we are members of any industry group that collects and shares operating information. This will enable us to compare our operating matrices and other important indicators to our peer group and will also help us to establish operating norms.

Sources of information:

Industry and trade associations
Professional associations (i.e., IEEE, IEC, ANSI, ISO, etc.)

We also want to be familiar with the third-party quality survey organization that independently test and report on our products and services. We want to know who our industry contact should be within these groups and become familiar with their survey techniques and information collection processes.

Sources of information:

Quality survey organizations

The purpose of phase 7 of our program has been to construct a system that enables us to recognize inputs from different information sources. We want to recognize both the quantitative and qualitative elements of our execution plans so that we can take corrective action should we have a need to do so.

Checklist

The scheduled receipt of operating statements
The scheduled receipt of market-segment virtual P&Ls
Establishment of implementation milestone reports
Establishment of product plan variance reporting
Recognition of independent test laboratories and their reports
Recognition of quality audit organizations and their impact
Recognition of business publications and our rankings

SUMMARY

There is no security on this earth. There is only opportunity.

—*General Douglas MacArthur*

We have discovered, organized, evaluated, qualified, and quantified an inordinate amount of information to develop our market plans. We must now pull it all together and construct a document that we can present to the C crowd that gives them confidence in our ability to accomplish these goals and objectives. There are various formats to consider in organizing this information, but we would like to suggest an approach that makes the document easier to understand. Many of the recipients of our plans may not have either a marketing or business background, so we have to tailor our document to the audience that is going to receive it.

We start with the suggested table of contents.

Executive Summary
Our Assumptions and Beliefs
Our Growth Opportunity
Our Goals and Objectives
Our Product and Sales Strategy
Our Financial Expectations
Our Governance Model

Executive Summary

Our summary needs to get right to the point and provide a synopsis of the following: our economic weather report; our market and industry size and its forecasted growth for the planning period; the identified needs within this market or industry we plan to address; the capabilities we will focus to satisfy these requirements; a summary of the products and services we plan to provide satisfying these needs. We intend to improve our market position from 10-percent market share to 20-percent market share within the five year planning horizon. Successful execution will result in revenue growth from our current $10 million per annum to $32 million per annum in year five. Our critical paths and financial requirements have been identified for successful implementation.

Stop here; no more detail in the summary.

Assumptions and Beliefs

The information we collected in phase 1 of our program is what we are going to summarize in this segment of our plan document. We are going to identify our place within the economy and share the actual data that supports our weather forecast. We are going to follow this information with our data analysis of our industry portraying the quantitative information we discovered that validate our growth projections. We will point out that the industry's projected growth provides a favorable opportunity for us to expand and that our conclusion from this analysis was that the timing is right for us to capture incremental market share.

Our Growth Opportunity

The market niches we identified are the opportunities that we are going to pursue, and they collectively have a quantitative value of X amount. We believe we can capture up to 20 percent of these purchase dollars because there is a definable need for the things that we provide or do. We will identify in this section any technology, cost, or business practice advantage that we believe would differentiate us from others in this market space. We will also acknowledge our major competitors and provide a short explanation as to why we feel that we can capture market share at a faster rate than they can, resulting in doubling our current market share. We are restating the business reasons we believe to support why we can compete and win in this environment.

Our Goals and Objectives

We are going to identify the targeted market segments we identified to capture. We will communicate any underserved markets we are planning to pursue that were identified in phase 3 of the program. We will also share any plans we may have to develop new products, enter new market segments, or expand to new geographies as part of our plans. What we need to convey to the C crowd is that our growth projections are based on a definitive plan to capture some identifiable segment of this targeted customer group. We are going to grow because we are now entering into segment C or geography X. Successful execution of this plan enables us to acquire an additional y number of customers that add a value to our business of z dollars.

Product and Sales Strategy

This segment of the plan document is going to support the goals and objectives we just summarized and to reinforce the tactics we just communicated. The information we collected in phase 4 of the program and the decisions we made in phase 5 are our data sources. We will also have a segment within this section that identifies our new product development plans. We need the C crowd to recognize how important this is to our success and make sure that they are aware of the investment support we are requesting. We are going to provide a quantitative summary of our entire product plan that provides anticipated units, revenues and margins. This information will be used by the C crowd to insure that other parts of the organization are prepared to support these new operational requirements.

We will also include a summary of our channel plans—the information we decided in phases 4 and 5 of the program. The C crowd is not interested in all of the gory details of this need, but they want to be comfortable that we have the market covered. We should provide summary data that informs them of the number of channels we plan to add and the new geographies we plan to cover. If we are contemplating a highly visible or strategic-distribution arrangement, we need to make that fact known. Any significant promotional plans we are considering should also be included in this section of the document so that when the media plans take hold, every member of the team is aware.

Financial Expectations

This section will include all of the financial information we developed and formatted in phase 5 and 6 of our program. It will have the standard chart of accounts populated with all of the quantifiable information we have to provide so that it can be easily uploaded into the company's overall operating budget. In addition, it needs to contain the virtual P&Ls by market segment that we developed in phase 6. We want these included so that the C crowd becomes comfortable with the manor in which we are planning to govern our efforts. We are tracking product, channel, and promotional costs in direct proportion to the impact they have on the markets we are trying to serve. Our accounting and finance groups will provide the templates we need to record these activities accurately.

Governance

We will be transferring the critical paths information we identified in phase 6 of the program into this segment. We will still recognize all of the quantitative goals we just communicated, but we also want to communicate our execution plans. We want the C crowd to understand that we have thought these requirements through and have a plan to insure that they are accomplished within the desired timelines. So, we need to develop a summary of the trees we developed in phase 6 that take the form of an engineering Gantt chart. These are the things we are going to accomplish in this order within these time frames in support of our market expansion objectives.

Many organizations do not require this section, but I have always felt that it is important. The senior management team needs to be comfortable that someone is watching the store other than the finance and control group. This is a good place to communicate the functional assignments we made within the marketing department and identify the owners of the critical paths we established in phase 6. What we are communicating in this section is recognition of the risks we are managing and the steps we are taking to mitigate these risks. Our early warning system has been established, and there are individuals assigned to each phase of the process to insure timely feedback and communication.

Congratulations! We now have assimilated the information we need to know, decided on a set of tactics for execution, and are ready to submit our official market plan document for approval.

CONCLUSION

Every morning in Africa, a gazelle wakes up. It knows it must run faster than the fastest lion, or it will be killed. Every morning a lion wakes up. It knows it must outrun the slowest gazelle, or it will starve to death. It doesn't matter whether you are a lion or a gazelle; when the sun comes up, you'd better be running.

—Unknown

We have now completed the cycle, albeit in record time, as the Targeted Tactics® workshop usually takes a full three days to complete. Our intent was to provide the reader with an organized process to develop a meaningful market plan that can be implemented and measured. We could not possibly address every issue in a generic manuscript of this nature, but we did our best to define a process to help you assimilate what you need to know. The specific enterprise content will always vary from industry to industry, company to company, but the disciplines and required steps that need to be followed are remarkably the same. I am confident in making that statement because the teams that I led were successful when we applied these disciplines, and conversely, we did not have success whenever we tried to shortcut the process.

I have not suggested in any segment of this manuscript that the Targeted Tactics® program replace the strategic planning process your organization may currently use. This program is designed to compliment your planning process and mitigate the implementation risks. The worst thing that can happen for any organization is to bet the farm on a new strategic direction only to later discover that it has stalled somewhere within the ranks. Targeted

Tactics® provides a measured and disciplined approach to the management of these marketing activities and should be viewed as complimentary, not confrontational. If we remember to incorporate these disciplines into the execution of our day to day responsibilities, then our contributions are going to continue to make a difference.

POST SCRIPT

I would be remiss if I did not have a few thoughts to share with the C crowd about their role in supporting this process. It seems that the senior teams can often be too quick to come to the wrong conclusions because they haven't taken enough time to ask the tough questions. Just because a market unit or an operating division is not performing up to expectations, does not necessarily mean that the business should be shut down and everybody sent home. There may be root causes that have led to this performance, and once they are discovered, corrective action can be taken to improve the situation and the outlook for these business areas.

Insist on investigating these root causes and challenge your management teams to exhaust their options and alternatives before closing things down. If your division general managers and marketing vice presidents can't answer the tough questions, then consider addressing this weakness within your organization. The telltale signs should be obvious; the weak ones will be quick to blame others for their shortfalls, and they will be unable to explain the actual dynamics occurring within their market environments. We do not need to have scorekeepers in these critical assignments; we need practitioners. The CFOs can keep score for all of us.

When I read today's business headlines, I admittedly remain concerned about the constant economic dislocation taking place within our economy. We rely on business and industry to provide us with the goods and services we need to sustain our society, and industry has a responsibility to recognize the importance of this role. Society is very dependent on industry's continued success to provide sustainable employment for our citizens and job creation to grow our economy. We can only fulfill this role by constantly reinventing ourselves and remaining competitive within the emerging global economy.

I leave the readers with a reason to care and a definitive process to work with. Utilize the tools provided in this book to help you understand your environment and your industry. Take the time to deliberately select the customers you want to serve. Review and modify your product plans annually so that you have the correct offerings to satisfy your customer's needs. Select the right channels and partners to represent your interests, and staff your support functions within affordable guidelines. Pick your targets of opportunity, and govern your efforts, not just measure the result. And finally, open up to the feedback of others so that you can truly understand your position within your market and your industry. Then make the adjustments that are necessary to sustain your organizations and remain competitive.

I sincerely hope that this book has helped, and I wish you the best of luck for continued success.

FOOTNOTES

The *Targeted Tactics® Program* has been assembled from many different sources of information that I have been able to learn from over the course of a lifetime. If I have neglected to acknowledge the original source of any of the concepts or ideas contained in this manuscript, I assure you that it was unintentional. I do not claim to be the originator of these thoughts, but rather the integrator, and I obviously have great appreciation for their value, or I would not have included them in this program.

Preface

Regis McKenna, *The Regis Touch: New Marketing Strategies for Uncertain Times*
Edward C. Bursk and William Morton, What is Marketing? Marketing
    Managers Handbook

Introduction

Charles M. Lillis, PhD, Del I. Hawkins, PhD, *Market Focus: Our Competitive Advantage*
Phillip Kotler, Marketing Management: Analysis, Planning, and Control

Phase 1 Determine Marketplace Environment

Yogi Berra, Berraisms
Lee Adler, Charles Mayer, Managing the Marketing Research Function
Alvin and Heidi Toffler, *Revolutionary Wealth,* Alfred A. Knopf, New York

United States Department of Commerce, US Census Bureau, Bureau of
    Economic Analysis, Economic Indicators Division
United States Office of Patents & Trademarks, *Summary of Patent Examining
    Activities*
United States Office of Management and Budget, *Fiscal Year 2007, MidSession
    Review*

Phase 2 Decide Nature of Company's Business

Geoffrey A. Moore, Crossing the Chasm
William E. Cox Jr., Product Life Cycles as Marketing Models
Michael E. Porter, Competitive Advantage—Creating and Sustaining Superior
    Performance

Phase 3 Identification of Customer Set

Geoffrey A. Moore, Crossing the Chasm
Abraham H. Maslow, A Theory of Human Motivation
William D. Wells, Psychographics: A Critical review
James F. Engle, Henry F. Fiorillo, Murray A. Cayley, *Market Segmentation,
    Concepts and Applications*
Thomas V. Bonoma, Benson Shapiro, *Industrial Market Segmentation*
Theodore Levitt, The Marketing Imagination
Richard R. Still, Segmenting the Market, Marketing Managers Handbook,
    Dartnell Press, Chicago, Ill.
Charles M. Lillis, PhD, Del I. Hawkins, PhD, *Market Focus: Our Competitive
    Advantage*

Phase 4 Determine Product and Sales Strategy

US Department of Commerce, Developing and Selling New Products
Walter B. Wentz and Gerald I. Eyrich, *Marketing: Theory and Application*
Thomas V. Bonoma, Robert A. Garda, *Industrial Marketing, Marketing
    Managers Handbook,* Dartnell Press, Chicago, Ill.
Theodore Levitt, The Marketing Imagination
Charles M. Lillis, PhD, Del I. Hawkins, PhD, *Market Focus: Our Competitive
    Advantage*
Geoffrey A. Moore, Crossing the Chasm
Donald M. Schrello, Product Evaluation and Planning

Frank R. Bacon Jr, Thomas W. Butler Jr., *Achieving Planned Innovation*

John L. Forbis, Nitin T. Mehta, Value-Based Strategies for Industrial Products

Allan J. Magrath, The 6 Imperatives of Marketing

William E. Cox Jr., Product Life Cycles as Marketing Models

Bob Lamons, The Case for B2B Branding

Phase 5 Organize and Apply Resources

Donald M. Schrello, Product Evaluation and Planning

Claire Corbin, John R. Sargent, Organization of the Marketing Department, Marketing Managers Handbook, Dartnell Press, Chicago, Ill.

Robert M. Tomasko, Re-Thinking the Corporation, The Architecture of Change

David A. Nadler, Michael L. Tushman, *Strategic Organization Design*

Peter F. Drucker, The Practice of Management

Harper W. Boyd Jr., Jean-Claude Larreche, *Setting Marketing Objectives, Marketing Managers Handbook,* Dartnell Press, Chicago, Ill.

Phillip Ward Burton, William Ryan, *Advertising Fundamentals*

Thomas V. Bonoma, Robert A. Garda, *Industrial Marketing, Marketing Managers Handbook,* Dartnell Press, Chicago, Ill.

Tony F. Allen, Critical Review of Sales Management Literature

Phase 6 Monitor and Measure Results

Robert D. Buzzell, Bradley T. Gale, and Ralph G. M. Sultan, *Market Share—A key to Profitability*

Theodore Levitt, Innovation in Marketing: New Perspective for Profit and Growth

Charles M. Lillis, PhD, Del I. Hawkins, PhD, *Market Focus: Our Competitive Advantage*

Robert L. Brintnall, George D. Mitchell, *Marketing Costs and Profits, Marketing Managers Handbook,* Dartnell Press, Chicago, Ill.

Analyzing and Improving Marketing Performance Report No 32, (New York American Management Association)

E. Jerome McCarthy, Durward Humes, *Marketing-Cost Analysis, Marketing Managers Handbook* Dartnell Press, Chicago, Ill.

Harold Kerzner, PhD, Project Management, a Systems Approach to Planning, Scheduling and Controlling

Phase 7 Feedback

Harold Kerzner, PhD, Project Management, a Systems Approach to Planning,
    Scheduling and Controlling
Joan Koob Cannie, Donald Caplan, Keeping Customers for Life
John C. Maxwell, The 21 Irrefutable Laws of Leadership
David H. Maister, Charles H. Green, Robert M. Galford, The Trusted
    Advisor
Consumer Reports Magazine
Underwriters Laboratory
Customer Satisfaction Measurement Association

INDEX